THE 6 STEPS TO
EMOTIONAL
FREEDOM

THE 6 STEPS TO EMOTIONAL FREEDOM

BREAKING THROUGH TO THE LIFE GOD WANTS YOU TO LIVE

DAVID CLARKE, PhD

BARBOUR
PUBLISHING

ISBN 978-1-59789-275-9

Throughout this book, names of individuals involved in the author's
counseling practice and/or program have been changed to protect privacy.

Cover design: The DesignWorks Group (www.thedesignworksgroup.com)

The author is represented by the literary agency of Hartline Marketing,
Pittsburgh, Pennsylvania.

Published by Barbour Publishing, Inc., P.O. Box 719, Uhrichsville, Ohio
44683, www.barbourbooks.com

*Our mission is to publish and distribute inspirational products offering excep-
tional value and biblical encouragement to the masses.*

Member of the
Evangelical Christian
Publishers Association

Printed in the United States of America.
5 4 3 2 1

To my mom, Kathleen Clarke,
a wonderful mother,
an extraordinary individual,
and the most emotionally healthy person I know.

CONTENTS

PART ONE:
THE TRUTH ABOUT EMOTIONAL PROBLEMS

PART TWO:
SIX STEPS TO EMOTIONAL AND SPIRITUAL HEALTH

Step One: Build Your Team

Step Two: Expose and Weaken Your Pattern

Step Three: Change Your Mind

Step Four: Express Your Emotions in a Healthy Way

Step Five: Face Your Unresolved Pain and Forgive

Step Six: Create a New Life

PART ONE

THE TRUTH ABOUT
EMOTIONAL PROBLEMS

CHAPTER 1

JOIN THE CLUB:
EVERYBODY HAS AN EMOTIONAL PROBLEM

The first words I say at one of my emotional-health seminars are designed to send a jolt of fear through my audience. I want those listening to feel nervous. I want them to sweat. I want them to fight the urge to cry out for their mamas. Believe me, that's exactly what happens.

When I take the stage I say this:

> *I'm going to begin with a brief demonstration. I'm a highly trained professional psychologist. I'm trained to identify and treat emotional problems. In fact, I'm so well trained I can actually tell if a person has an emotional problem by just looking at him or her. I will now point out those of you who have emotional problems.*

At this point, I leave the stage and walk right into the audience. I stroll slowly down the center aisle, scanning the crowd carefully. There's a lot of nervous laughter, and you can cut the intensity in the room with a knife. Suddenly, every single person present has a serious case of ants in the pants. There's more fidgeting going on than in a kindergarten class. Bottoms are squirming, eyes are darting, and lips are licking.

I can see from their panicked expressions what people are thinking:

Is this guy crazy?
He's not serious, is he?

Does he have some kind of special powers?

Maybe if I can look normal, he'll pass me over.

Mama! Help me, Mama!

I know I shouldn't have worn this purple lipstick; he'll think I'm nuts for sure.

I think he's *the one with the emotional problem!*

The next words out of my mouth put everyone at ease: "Actually, it's very easy. *You all do.* Every person in this room, including me, has an emotional problem."

The fear and nail-biting anxiety evaporate. All the tension washes out of the room with a beautiful *whoosh.* With three simple words—*"You all do"*—I have connected with my audience. I have communicated what they desperately needed to hear: We're all in this together.

There's No Such Thing as Normal

I get a kick out of newspaper and magazine articles that talk about the incidence of emotional problems in Americans. They'll say: "Four out of every ten Americans will have an emotional problem at some point in their lives." Some articles will even go as high as five or six out of ten. I say baloney. Ten out of ten Americans already have an emotional problem. You don't have to wait to get one. You have one right now!

The only person who ever lived on earth who did not have an emotional problem was Jesus Christ. He suffered terrible pain and experienced depression and anxiety but never developed an emotional problem. He was—and is—the healthiest person in the history of the world.

You're not Jesus. You have an emotional problem.

One of the central and most dangerous myths in both Christian and secular culture is that only certain unfortunate individuals have serious emotional problems. A bad childhood, genetic predisposition, or a series of poor choices cause some people to be messed up. They're abnormal and need to work hard on their issues. We feel sorry for them, pray for them, and hope they can get their lives back on track.

Most of us truly believe we are normal. Oh, we normal sorts don't think we're perfect. We do have some minor or major struggles in certain areas. We're clever enough to admit the obvious. But we think we're pretty much okay. Especially compared to those poor, emotionally troubled souls who *really* have significant problems.

As a Christian psychologist in private practice since 1986, I've seen thousands of clients in my therapy office. I haven't seen a normal one yet. By normal, I mean the absence of a serious problem. I've spoken with thousands of people during my marriage, parenting, and emotional-health seminars. Not one has been normal. I don't have one single member of my family who is normal. None of my friends are normal. I'm not normal. No one is.

Every person I've ever met in my life has a serious emotional problem. A problem that, if not properly addressed, will do terrible damage.

Why You Have an Emotional Problem
Now that I've told you that you have an emotional problem and that you're not normal, I won't leave you hanging. You need to know why you have your problem. A simple formula explains it: Clarke's Universal Formula for Emotional Disturbance, CUFFED for short. You know, I always wanted something named after me, and it just wasn't happening. So I named this formula after myself.

Old Nature + Needs + Pain = Emotional Disturbance

The first element in my formula is *old nature*. The Bible describes human beings as selfish, deceitful, and totally focused on self. Me, me, me, me. And me some more. We don't learn to be selfish. We're all born that way. Romans 1:25 drives this point home with a sickening crunch: "For they exchanged the truth of God for a lie, and worshiped and served the creature rather than the Creator."

The *they* in that verse means *us*. By nature, we worship ourselves!

Being this incredibly selfish is bad enough. But it's worse than that. The Bible—in the first three chapters of the book of Romans and many other places—teaches that by nature we distort the truth, we think wicked thoughts, and we behave in sinful ways.

Jeremiah 17:9 provides a powerful summary of our old nature: "The heart is more deceitful than all else and is desperately sick; who can understand it?"

The second element in my formula is *needs*. We're all born with needs. God-given needs. We all have a desperate need to be loved—to feel as though we belong, to be intimate with someone, to be unconditionally accepted. We all have a deep need to be valued—to feel worthy, to have respect, and to be competent. We carry these needs around every day of our lives. We do whatever we can to get these essential needs met and to avoid rejection.

Old nature plus *needs* leads to a tremendous focus on self. From birth, we think we're the center of the universe, and we spend all of our time trying to get our needs met. We also tend to think in distorted ways and naturally gravitate to sinful behaviors. The stage is set.

The third element in my formula, *pain*, leads to emotional disturbance. Pain is any threat to my needs. No parents are perfect, and so needs are not met. Emotional pain occurs. And it doesn't stop with parents. We all experience serious psychological pain growing up in our homes, in our neighborhoods, in our schools, on playgrounds and sporting fields, at the mall, through the media, and in countless other places where we feel the sting of disappointment, neglect, rejection, and possibly abuse.

It's an unbeatable combination. It's a universal experience. No one escapes. You have an old nature which forces you to be selfish, to think inaccurately, and to behave sinfully. You have critically important needs that you yearn to meet. When pain enters your world, you begin to develop a plan to cope with that pain and get your needs met. Because of your old nature, this plan will be unhealthy. But it's the best you can do. For now.

What's Your Problem?

Let's get specific. Given your family, your past experiences, and your personality, how do you cope with pain and try to get your needs met?

What's your particular emotional problem?

Are you depressed? Anxious? Angry? An alcoholic? A drug addict? A sex addict? A homosexual? A workaholic? A shopaholic? A gambler? Obese? Anorexic? Bulimic? A perfectionist? Obsessive-compulsive? Full of self-hate?

Are you a victim of physical, verbal, or sexual abuse? An unrecovered victim of rape? Have you had an abortion, gone through a divorce, or experienced a broken relationship? Do you lack forgiveness?

Do you love money? Fame? Power? Control?

Are you jealous? A chronic liar? A thief? Prideful? Lazy? Greedy? A gossip? Financially irresponsible? A constant complainer? A dependent people-pleaser?

Are you a doormat, a clown, a wallflower, or a rescuer?

You're somewhere on that list, aren't you? And it's not a complete list by any stretch. Maybe you're on the list in more than one area of struggle. I'm on the list. I'm a workaholic. My work habits have hurt me, hurt my marriage, hurt my kids, and hurt my effectiveness for Christ.

Every one of us has an emotional problem. I'm not okay and neither are you. Your emotional problem isn't just a minor annoyance, either. It's serious. Deadly serious. It's already crippled you, and will destroy you if you don't follow the right recovery plan. There is a way to emotional health, and I'm going to show you what it is.

Definition of Emotional Problem

Here's exactly what you have: an ingrained pattern of faulty thinking, unhealthy emotional expression, and sinful behavior which helps you cope with pain and meet your needs but that actually cripples all your relationships and gives Satan a foothold in your life.

An Ingrained Pattern

Your problem is something you do over and over again. It's a way of life. It has deep roots that go back a long way. It began with pain as a child, grew with pain as a teenager, and solidified into a pattern in young adulthood. You don't suddenly and mysteriously develop an emotional problem. A traumatic event as a teen or adult can worsen your emotional problem and bring it to a more life-disrupting level. But your problem was already there.

Faulty Thinking

By nature, you already distort the truth. Painful events occur in your childhood and teen years, and you don't have the intellectual maturity and ability to process them and think accurately about them. You reach incorrect, negative conclusions about yourself, others, and God. These incorrect thoughts shape how you see yourself and how you interact with others.

Unhealthy Emotional Expression

You learn to keep your true feelings to yourself. It's too painful and embarrassing to reveal them to anyone. You don't want to be that vulnerable and exposed. Or you may have been told that it is wrong to express negative feelings. Stuffing your true, deep emotions or spewing them out in an explosive way creates tremendous intensity inside. They must be expressed somehow. No one ever taught you how to express your emotions in a healthy way.

Sinful Behavior

The end result of faulty thinking and stuffed emotions is sinful behavior. Your internal intensity and pain is forced out in the form of sinful behavior. This relieves the tension temporarily, but it harms you and begins a whole new cycle of faulty thinking, unhealthy emotional expression, and sinful behavior. Sinful behavior doesn't just happen. It's always the inevitable result of faulty thinking and unhealthy emotional expression.

Coping with Pain

When pain strikes you as a child and teenager, you're not mature enough—intellectually or spiritually—to handle these wounds in a healthy, productive way. You find a pattern that seems to offer some protection and ease the pain. Your behavior pattern does provide temporary relief and distracts you from the pain. In reality, your coping style increases your pain. Instead of facing your pain directly, you run from it. Your method of pain management doesn't work, but you continue to use it, because it's all you know.

Meeting Your Needs

You're born with God-given needs to be loved and valued. As you grow up, these important needs are not all met and you experience the pain of fear, insecurity, and a damaged self-image. Since others are not meeting your needs, you take matters into your own hands. You create a system, a strategy that serves the dual purpose of escaping the pain and satisfying your needs. However, rather than fulfilling your needs, your flawed strategy intensifies them.

Crippling Your Relationships

Your dysfunctional style of coping with pain and meeting needs saps your time, energy, and vitality. It keeps you feeling guilty, worthless, and burdened. It draws you away from the people who can genuinely meet your needs. Instead of spending time enriching your relationships, you spend time feeding your emotional problem. Your sinful behavior harms you and those who love you. Worst of all, your emotional problem blocks you from a close, growing relationship with God.

Giving Satan a Foothold

Your emotional problem provides Satan with an avenue into your life. If you know Christ personally, Satan cannot possess you. But he can and will use your emotional problem to harass and damage you.

Your emotional problem, your damaging pattern of thinking and emotional expression and behavior, is in place and likely operating at full strength well before you begin a relationship with Jesus Christ. Even after you know Jesus, your old nature—and the old pattern connected to it—remains. With Jesus in your life, you now have the power to defeat your pattern and live a healthy, victorious life, but it will take work and the right steps of recovery.

Hall of Shame to Hall of Fame

In chapter 11 of Hebrews, Paul (in my opinion, he wrote the book) gives us the famous biblical Hall of Fame. He describes the godly, faithful behavior of the giants of the Old Testament. Every single person mentioned had an emotional problem. They all had issues! They all sinned and made serious mistakes. As we battle to overcome our emotional problems, we can take heart. We're in good company. Very good company.

Check out these Hall of Famers and their emotional problems:

- *Abraham:* fearful, cowardly, a liar, and self-protective;

- *Sarah:* sharp tongued, sarcastic, unsatisfied, jealous, and unforgiving;

- *Jacob:* selfish, a thief, hateful, and obsessive of his brother;

- *Joseph:* spoiled, arrogant, insensitive, an inflated self-perception. He was such a pain his brothers plotted to kill him;

- *Moses:* poor self-esteem, angry, violent, impatient, impetuous;

- *Rahab:* shamed, self-loathing, distorted view of men;

- *Samson:* sexual addict, lustful, prideful;

- *David:* self-centered, lustful, an adulterer, a liar, a murderer.

How in the world did seriously flawed individuals like these end up in the Hall of Fame? Four reasons. God loved them. God had great plans for them. God was patient with them. And

I believe each of them—with God's help and power—*worked hard on their weaknesses* and *truly changed*. If these troubled souls can overcome their emotional problems and grow into healthy servants of God, so can we.

Every one of these giants of the faith went through testing, pain, and character building. In every case, the transformation from emotional basket case to godly warrior did not occur quickly and easily. There were no instantaneous miracles of healing. God could have done it that way, but He didn't. God chose to lead each one down a road of recovery that involved time, effort, and perseverance. At the end of the journey, each came through to a deep level of emotional wholeness and faith in the living God. So can we.

The Road to Emotional Health

I want to show you the end of the road. The destination you want to reach. Here's my definition of emotional health: an ingrained pattern of accurate thinking, healthy emotional expression, and godly behavior that helps you cope with pain and meet your needs, enriches all your relationships, and keeps Satan from being effective in your life.

I know you want to get healthy. That's why you're reading this book.

The good news is, there is a way to heal and become emotionally whole. I'm going to explain, step by specific step, exactly how to do it.

My recovery approach is not the one recommended and taught by the leading Christian "experts" of today. These best-selling authors, pastors, Christian psychologists, and radio personalities are well meaning, but their principles don't work. If you attempt to follow the popular Christian approaches to emotional problems, you're likely doomed to fail. Many of you have already tried one or more of these popular strategies, and you're still stuck with your emotional problem.

As a next step in communicating how my recovery program works, I'll explain why these other approaches are unable to produce real, lasting change.

Do Your Work

1. What is your emotional problem?

2. How is it impacting your life? Career? Marriage? Parenting? Relationship with God?

3. Which biblical Hall of Famer do you identify with the most?

4. How did this biblical person's emotional problem impact his or her life?

5. How did his or her story turn out?

6. Are you finally sick enough of your problem to do the hard work to get control of it?

7. Pray—right now—that God will give you the courage and the power to do what you have to do to heal.

CHAPTER 2

HEALING IS HARD WORK:
EMOTIONAL PROBLEMS REQUIRE
MORE THAN SPIRITUAL SOLUTIONS

I was in my car, returning to my office after lunch. I was listening to a national Christian radio show. The guest that day was a best-selling author and well-known conference speaker. If I wrote his name, you'd probably know him.

The topic of the show was forgiveness. I said out loud to myself, "This ought to be interesting." After making a few comments about how important forgiveness is and how God commands us to forgive—both true—he said something that almost made me lose control of my car.

He told the host and the national radio audience that if he could spend one hour with a person, that person would leave his office having totally and completely forgiven whoever had hurt him. He said it didn't make any difference what kind of wound it was or how long ago it had happened.

All that person had to do was realize it was a spiritual problem with a spiritual solution. One heartfelt prayer asking God to heal the pain and provide the power to forgive would get the job done. Instant healing. That person would walk out of his office fully released from resentment and able to confidently move ahead in life.

I waved my arms and began talking to the radio: "No, that's not right! I really wish it were, but it's not! You don't forgive that way! Forgiveness takes time, effort, and the right steps. Emotional problems aren't *just* spiritual problems. It takes more than simple faith to solve them. Yes, of course, God will heal you, but He'll almost always require you to work hard, and it will take a lot longer than one hour!"

As I talked and gestured at my car radio, I noticed several other drivers staring at me with concerned looks on their faces. They were looking at me as though I were a crazy man. One lady was clutching her cell phone, and I thought maybe she was getting ready to call the police or the men in the white coats. I almost rolled down my window to say, "I'm a Christian psychologist. It's okay!" Instead, I just drove to my office to do more of the work that actually does heal hurting people.

The Popular Christian Way Is the Wrong Way

This Christian leader on the radio is a good and godly man. He loves Jesus and is truly trying to help others. He's well-meaning and sincere. But sincerity doesn't always equal accuracy. His belief that anyone can instantly be healed of serious past wounds with a three-sentence prayer—or in one hour—is incorrect.

Unfortunately, he is smack-dab in the middle of the mainstream Christian view of emotional problems. His teachings on how to forgive are an accurate snapshot of the Christian community's approach to solving emotional problems. His message, and the message of most other influential Christian experts, is that emotional problems are spiritual problems and so require *only* a spiritual solution.

These Christian authorities believe strongly that having a relationship with Jesus Christ is all you need to experience quick and total recovery from any problem. On national radio shows, in best-selling books, in Christian magazines, and in seminars, they tell you that knowing and trusting Jesus shortens the healing process or eliminates it altogether. All you have to do to completely heal from past abuse, an addiction, or any emotional problem, is claim the power of Jesus in a brief prayer.

Their message sounds good. It sounds right. It sounds Christian. I've spoken with high-profile Christian leaders who teach quick and easy spiritual problem solving. They're terrific people. They're kind and caring, and they love Jesus. They're making a heartfelt attempt to help hurting individuals. But they do not understand how true, deep healing happens.

There Is a Better Way
For almost twenty years, ever since I received my PhD in psychology, I've been waiting for the Christian community to get it right. I was sure that eventually people in highly visible positions would figure out how emotional problems get healed. But they haven't figured it out yet. The Christian experts are still saying the same old things.

So I've decided to speak up and share what God has taught me about healing emotional problems. I'm going to tell you the truth, based on the Bible and my twenty years of clinical practice and my personal experiences, about what causes emotional problems and exactly how the healing process works. I hope and pray and believe this book will lead you to true recovery and a close, dynamic walk with Jesus Christ.

The Truth
The fact of the matter is, healing is hard work. Yes, God is intimately involved in recovery. He provides the power to heal. Even when your faith in Him is weak, God hangs in there with you and gets you through. But healing from your emotional problem is a process that involves time, effort, and specific steps. God will not zap you and heal you immediately. God will help you do your work. Remember: He could have changed how your life experiences led you to where you are; He chose not to do that. Emotional problems are not, at their core, spiritual problems.

They are emotionally created and driven and so require emotional as well as spiritual solutions. Emotional problems have deep psychological roots that must be exposed and ripped out. The spiritual is involved, with Satan playing a part, and God always present. Satan will use your emotional struggle to enter your life and harass you. God will heal you and, at the same time, build your spiritual life and character through the journey of recovery.

Healing Isn't Fast

If you follow the Christian community's logic, you'd say to a person with a damaged heart muscle: "This is a spiritual problem. You don't need to see a medical doctor. Your faith in God can make you well. Pray and God will heal you."

Well, of course the person ought to pray. God wants prayer in this kind of a situation. And yes, God will do the healing. But the heart problem, at its core, is a physical problem. It will require physical solutions: drugs, heart catheterization, surgery, exercise, diet, and lifestyle changes.

If He chooses, God will perform the healing of the damaged heart. He'll use the doctor's skill and specific physical procedures to restore health. Along the way, He'll teach the wounded person critical life lessons through the period of recovery.

The Christian experts on emotional problems would read my heart example and immediately protest: "But a damaged heart is much different from an emotional problem. It's obvious that a diseased heart muscle requires physical intervention."

My response is, "No, an injured heart and an emotional problem are very much alike. Both take years to develop. Both do not grow out of spiritual weakness or lack of faith. God will heal both, but their solutions will not be primarily spiritual. The heart will demand physical steps of healing. The emotional problem will demand emotional steps of healing."

God rarely provides immediate healing. He certainly can. He can do anything. Why doesn't He? Because He wants you to learn from the difficult process of healing. Your heavenly Father wants you to grow, build new character, and change in healthy ways. If you were suddenly and miraculously healed, you wouldn't learn a thing.

For the past year, we have been going through an extremely painful, heartbreaking ordeal with someone close to our family. This loved one is battling a serious physical and psychological disorder. Have my wife and I prayed for healing? You'd better believe it. Over and over and over again. Has God healed quickly? No. The nightmare, with all its pain and anguish, is still going on. We're going through it with our friend, guided and helped by medical and psychological professionals. God is with us and, aided by His grace and support, we're all learning and changing and growing.

I want this precious person healed. Now. Today would be good. But God's way is almost always the long and narrow and tough way. It also happens to be the best way.

Why the Experts Are Wrong

I've contradicted the Christian experts in general terms. Now, I'm going to get specific. Their central belief—that emotional problems are primarily, or solely, spiritual problems—comes in five major variations. Here they are, along with my explanation of why they're wrong:

It's a Faith Issue

> *Because your problem is a spiritual problem, the answer to it is to grow spiritually. You are unable*

*to overcome it, because your faith is weak. You're not
close enough to God. You're not trusting Him enough.
Work hard on your spiritual life: Have more quiet
times; read the Bible; memorize verses; deepen your
prayer life. Then your problem will disappear.*

This approach sounds spiritual, but it's not accurate and causes unnecessary feelings of guilt. The Christians who teach this message don't know how healing actually takes place. They tell you that you are struggling because you don't love God enough. You're a lousy Christian with mediocre faith. If you were more spiritual, you'd be healthy.

This argument has been used for centuries, and it's never been true. It was bogus when it was first invented, and it's bogus now. Faith alone won't eliminate your emotional problem. Faith will certainly be involved in the process. It's the most important part of life and impacts every aspect of your existence, but faith alone is not the central healing mechanism.

How can I say that? Because of the example of the apostle Paul. He was the most godly, faith-filled Christian in the early church. He wrote three-quarters of the New Testament. He had a deep, intimate faith in God. No one has ever walked closer to Jesus. It's possible that no one has ever lived a life more connected to the power of the Holy Spirit. No one. And yet read Paul's words: "For what I am doing, I do not understand; for I am not practicing what I would like to do, but I am doing the very thing I hate. . . . For the good that I want, I do not do, but I practice the very evil that I do not want" (Romans 7:15, 19).

Can you believe it? Paul struggled just as we do! If you have the perspective of the Christian experts, his faith was too weak. Don't you believe it. Paul's faith was stronger than yours or mine or anyone else's, and it still wasn't enough to defeat his problem.

If faith alone wasn't enough for Paul, it won't be enough for you and me.

God wants your faith to be built up by going through the struggle of recovery. But faith alone won't solve the problem. There's emotional work to be done.

Claim Your Position and Power in Christ

> As a Christian, you are a new creature. You possess all you need in Christ. Christ has already achieved the victory. All you have to do is claim it for yourself in His power. In a brief prayer, just accept the healing Jesus has provided through His death, resurrection, and ongoing presence in your life.

The proponents of this spiritual solution are right about your position and power in Christ. The moment you believe Jesus died for your sins and rose from the dead, you become a new creature, and you have access to His infinite power.

But these spiritual advisors are wrong about how you use that power to become a healthy person. Simply claiming Christ's healing power won't get the job done. I wish it would, but it won't.

There are emotional and psychological obstacles to getting Christ's power and using it. For example, I met with a woman who had been sexually and emotionally abused as a child by her father. This unresolved pain is blocking her from a close relationship with God, her heavenly Father. She'll have to remove this obstacle before she can truly trust God and Jesus.

Merely claiming the power of Jesus won't heal this dear lady. What will heal her is claiming the power of Jesus to help her do the hard work of recovery. She is a new creature now, even before she begins the recovery process. She will feel like a new creature and act like a new creature after she and Jesus work through the pain of her past.

Philippians 4:13 is a verse I use with many of my clients: "I can do all things through Him who strengthens me." The word *Him* refers to Jesus Christ. The phrase *all things* includes your emotional problem. *Strengthens* means Jesus will give you the power you need to work your recovery program and become a vital, healthy follower of His.

Go Through a Healing Ceremony

> *You can be completely healed in a one-time spiritual ceremony. Gather together with two or three other faithful Christians and pray that God will heal you. Take your past wounds and your current problems to the cross and give them to Jesus. Jesus will take your burdens, and you will walk away totally free from your pain and its influence on your life.*

Let me be clear. I believe healing ceremonies like these can be an important part of the recovery process. I love—and have used—the image of giving your wounds to Jesus. But rituals like these are not enough on their own. I have a suspicion that those Christian leaders who recommend these ceremonies fear the real pain, intensity, and anguish of the recovery process, so they detour around it with a healing ceremony.

Wouldn't it be easier if Jesus would heal through a spiritual prayer meeting like this? It sure would be. I'd be the first one in line to take advantage of a quick, microwave-fast recovery. But Jesus doesn't operate that way.

Healing takes months. It doesn't happen quickly. Of course,

Jesus can heal in an instant. But He doesn't do that in the vast majority of cases. Jesus will heal you, but He'll take you on a difficult, painful road to get there. He wants you to build faith and character—which requires time and work and sacrifice.

Again and again in the New Testament (Romans 5, James 1, 1 Peter 1), we are taught that the Christian life includes suffering. There is no other way to build a genuinely strong, dynamic spirituality. I'm convinced one part of this suffering is working on the emotional problem that comes with it. The process will be hard work and it will hurt, but it will be worth it.

Why would God allow you to develop an emotional problem and then, suddenly and miraculously, heal you from it? He wouldn't do that. God will deal with you the same way He dealt with the members of the Hebrews 11 Hall of Fame. Remember them from chapter 1? Every single Hall of Famer suffered. Every single one had to be dragged through a process of maturation and change. Every single one had to work hard on personal emotional issues over time. And every single one fought through to a victorious life of faith.

You could be next.

You're Sinning. Stop It!

> *I don't want to hear any mumbo-jumbo about a bad childhood, poor self-esteem, or addiction. That's all psychobabble invented by godless men who didn't believe in the Bible and just made it up. You don't have an emotional problem. You've got a sin problem. Your behavior is sinful, and you're choosing to continue in your sin. The answer is to stop sinning and obey God.*

This variation has all the subtlety of a shovel to the head. It's rude. It's offensive. It's damaging. Emotional problems do exist. They do involve sinful behavior, and we are fallen creatures with a sin nature. However, they are far more complicated than this simplistic view asserts. Emotional problems have deep, tangled roots, and only hard work can kill them.

The apostle Paul couldn't just stop his sinful behavior, could he? It really had a grip on him, and he was man enough—and Christian enough—to admit it. If we could just stop our sinful behaviors, there would be no process of sanctification.

Most of my clients don't want to sin. If they could stop sinning, they would. They come to see me because they have tried to stop their destructive behavior and have failed time after time. They're caught in their pattern. With God's help and power, we work together to expose their pattern, find out how it works, and do the work necessary to dismantle it. That's therapy, and it's a whole lot more effective than saying, "Stop sinning, right now."

It's Spiritual Warfare

> *Your problem is the result of satanic warfare. Satan, through his demons, is attacking you and exerting a certain level of control over your life. Jesus has the power to drive out the demons and release you from bondage. What you need is an exorcism in which the demons are ordered out by the authority of Jesus Christ and His shed blood. When the demons leave, so will your problem.*

As with the previous four variations of the spiritual solution, this one contains truth. But like all the rest, the truth is incomplete and therefore misleading. Demonic activity certainly can be involved in emotional problems, but it's rarely the main force that gives them life. An exorcism will not be enough to heal you.

Demons can and do wield influence through your emotional problem. They get into your life by means of your emotional problem (2 Corinthians 2:11; Ephesians 4:26–27), and then they use it to harass, cripple, and eventually destroy you. The demons cannot possess you if you have a personal relationship with Jesus Christ, but they can brutalize and torment you as long as your emotional problem is in place and operating. When your emotional problem is resolved, they lose their foothold and can easily be dismissed.

I saw a young woman some years ago who had been horribly abused as a child. As a result, she was seriously depressed and had multiple personalities. An exorcism at the beginning of the therapy process wouldn't have worked. The demons harassing her were firmly attached to her unresolved past pain. Once she had worked through her abuse, the demons lost their stronghold and, using the authority of Jesus Christ, we quickly flushed them out. The process, however, was long and demanding and painful for the woman.

You Must Do Your Work
I've explained how the popular Christian approach to healing is wrong. Now it's time to show you the right way to heal. My approach, which I believe is strongly supported by scripture, is based on Philippians 2:12–13: "So then, my beloved, just as you have always obeyed, not as in my presence only, but now much more in my absence, work out your salvation with fear and trembling; for it is God who is at work in you, both to will and to work for His good pleasure."

We don't work for our salvation, which is a free gift through faith (Ephesians 2:8–9). But we most certainly do work on our spiritual growth, and relationship with Jesus Christ. This process is known as sanctification, and it's hard work. Taking the difficult and often painful steps to heal from an emotional problem is an integral part of sanctification. God uses our emotional problem and the recovery process to mold us and make us more like His Son, Jesus Christ.

God will always do His part in the recovery process. He'll provide the guidance, the power, the comfort, the encouragement, the insight, and the endurance we need.

We have to do our part by working through the six steps of healing:

Step One: Build Your Team
No one ever changes and heals alone. No one. A team gives you strength, accountability, and motivation. With Jesus, one close friend, and a local church body, you have the team members needed to successfully travel on the healing journey.

Step Two: Expose and Weaken Your Pattern
True healing begins by taking a good, hard look at your patterns of thinking, emotional expression, and behavior. Orally and in writing, you'll lay bare the details of how you operate in your area of weakness. When you know precisely how a mechanism works, you can interrupt its flow and tear it apart.

Step Three: Change Your Mind
Your inaccurate, negative, and unbiblical thinking is a key component of your emotional problem. You must identify and eliminate your bad thinking and replace it with healthy, positive, and biblical thinking.

Step Four: Express Your Emotions in a Healthy Way

When you learn how to express your emotions—including anger—in four ways and deal with stress, your emotional system will run more smoothly and you'll be able to build intimacy in your relationships.

Step Five: Face Your Unresolved Pain and Forgive

Your pain from the past transfers to the present and attacks all of your personal relationships. Orally and in writing, you'll deal directly with those who caused you harm (family, friends, others) and those you have harmed. This work is the only way to truly forgive others and feel forgiven for your past mistakes.

Step Six: Create a New Life

It's time to live. Really live. With the chains of your emotional problem broken, you can now create the kind of life God wants you to enjoy. You'll grow spiritually, you'll use your God-given gifts and talents in His service, you'll build intimate relationships with those you love, and you'll make a difference in the world.

I believe God has allowed me to develop a plan of recovery that works. It gets at the roots of emotional problems. It addresses the emotional and spiritual dimensions of healing. It's how I've worked with hurting people for twenty years. It's proven. It's reliable. It's effective. It brings glory to God.

If you're serious about getting healthy, let's get to work.

Do Your Work

1. Before reading this chapter, what did you believe about how emotional problems operate and how to heal from them?

2. Which of the five variations of the popular Christian teaching on emotional problems (Why the Experts Are Wrong) has influenced you the most? Where did you encounter this teaching? Did you try to follow it and, if so, how did you do?

3. Why do you think God hasn't healed you yet from your emotional problem?

4. What are your fears as you prepare to read about the six steps of healing?

5. What has stopped you from doing the hard work of healing? Not knowing the right way? Bad advice from a pastor, counselor, or author? Your own lack of motivation? Going it alone without any support from others? Something else?

PART TWO

_____

SIX STEPS TO EMOTIONAL AND SPIRITUAL HEALTH

CHAPTER 3

YOUR TRIED AND TRUE TEAM: ACCOUNTABILITY, SUPPORT, AND LOVE

Remember that amazing day some years ago when one man, completely on his own, reached the summit of Mount Everest? That intrepid adventurer did what no one had ever done before. He defied all the experts who said it was impossible. Armed with only his loaded backpack and a fierce glint in his eye, he conquered mighty Everest by himself.

I know he's someone you'll never forget. The picture he took of himself at the top of the tallest mountain on earth is burned into all our memories. The image of his crazy grin, icicle-encrusted beard, and T-shirt with the words WHO NEEDS HELP? was on the front page of every newspaper in the world.

He was all over television. He did all the morning and evening news shows. He was a guest on all the late night and cable talk shows. He visited the White House and slept in the Lincoln bedroom. He basked in the glory of a ticker tape parade in New York City. Barbara Walters made him cry when she asked about his favorite pick snapping in two just one hundred yards from the peak.

Wait a minute. You don't remember this? Well, of course you don't. It never happened. I'm pulling your leg. No one has ever climbed Mount Everest alone. No one ever will. It's far too difficult for one person. Many have reached the top of Everest, but they've always done it as part of a team. This massive mountain can only be scaled by teams of climbers.

No One Ever Heals Alone

Your problem isn't Mount Everest, but it's a pretty big mountain. No one ever heals alone. No one. You need help to conquer your emotional problem. You always heal in relationship. Always. No exceptions. Don't waste your time trying to recover alone. You'll never make it.

The phrase *one another* is found fifty-eight times in the New Testament. Fifty-eight times! God makes it clear that we need each other. I could fill an entire book with all the verses in the Bible instructing us to support, love, encourage, confront, and be accountable to each other.

Ecclesiastes 4:9–12 is clear: "Two are better than one because they have a good return for their labor. For if either of them falls, the one will lift up his companion. But woe to the one who falls when there is not another to lift him up. Furthermore, if two lie down together they keep warm, but how can one be warm alone? And if one can overpower him who is alone, two can resist him. A cord of three strands is not quickly torn apart."

The first step on your journey of healing is to create your support team. It's what God wants you to do. It's the foundation of your success.

There are two essential team members and three more who are beneficial to have.

Your Accountability Partner

You need one person, of the same sex, who will walk with you on the rocky road of recovery. With you. Not behind you. Not ahead of you. Right beside you. This person will know everything about your emotional problem. What you've done. What you've thought. Your struggles. Your temptations. How your problem impacts your spiritual life, your work life, and your family life.

You'll tell your accountability partner everything you've done in your area of weakness in the past; everything you're doing, thinking, and feeling in the present; and what your plans are for the future. Your accountability partner will know all the nasty truth. . .and will still love you unconditionally. Your partner will tell no one—no one—your secrets. Your partner will be loyal, speak the truth, comfort you, encourage you, yell at you when necessary, be available to you, pray with you, and hold you accountable.

This is an intense, personal, and intimate relationship. It creates an emotional and spiritual bond. And it will change your life.

James knows what I'm talking about. "Therefore, confess your sins to one another, and pray for one another so that you may be healed. The effective prayer of a righteous man can accomplish much" (James 5:16). How about that for an endorsement of an accountability relationship?

What a powerful message! James gives us a bold, direct prescription for recovery: Confess your sins to another, pray together about those sins, and healing can take place. Simple. Clear. Effective. Relying on your accountability partner in these spiritual ways will be an integral part of your recovery process.

Solomon knows what I'm talking about. He knows the kind of person who makes the best accountability partner: "A friend loves at all times, and a brother is born for adversity" (Proverbs 17:17).

You're looking for someone who will be there with you when times are tough. When you're in pain. When you're in crisis. When you get serious about working on your emotional problem.

You've heard the saying about true friends, haven't you? "When you're in trouble, you find out who your real friends are." That is 100 percent true. There are plenty of people who are gutless wonders. Weasels. Good time, superficial, and pseudofriends who will cut and run when you need help. What you need is a friend who will stick with you in good times and bad. A fellow warrior who will stand beside you and fight as the battles rage.

You Need a Jonathan

David found that kind of a friend in Jonathan, a man who loved him without reservations, without excuses, and without any conditions (1 Samuel 18:1–4).

Jonathan was in an impossible situation. His father, King Saul, hated David and wanted him dead. Jonathan had to side with his father and distance himself from David, didn't he? No, he didn't. At tremendous risk, he remained loyal to David (1 Samuel 19:1–7).

God supports accountability relationships. In addition to specific teaching on developing relationships that are intimate and accountable, there are many examples in the Bible of this kind of unique friendship. In addition to Jonathan and David, here are others:

- Moses and Joshua;

- Ruth and Naomi;

- Samuel and David;

- Elijah and Elisha;

- Mary, Jesus' mother, and Elizabeth, John the Baptist's mother;

- Mary and Martha, sisters of Lazarus;

• Paul and Barnabas;

• Paul and Timothy.

There are few Lone Rangers in the pages of scripture. Just about every significant, influential person in the Bible has a sidekick. A close associate. A key right-hand man or woman. You need one, too. Hey, even the Lone Ranger had Tonto.

The Man from Ludowici

I'm not going to tell you to do anything I'm not doing. I have an accountability partner. You've heard of the man from Snowy River. Well, this is the man from Ludowici. It's a small town in Georgia where they grow their men with strong backs and weak minds—at least, that's how he describes it. This man also happens to be my business associate and best friend. His name is Roscoe D. Glisson. I call him Rocky. I can't call a man Roscoe. I'm sorry, I just can't do it.

Rocky and I have developed a James 5:16 relationship. We tell each other the truth. We confess our sins to each other. We pray for each other. I know his weaknesses, and he knows mine.

We are experiencing the tremendous power and motivation of a relationship in which there is complete openness and honesty. No secrets. No walls. No games. No faking. No false fronts.

What we have is the ability to say this: "Here is who I am and how my life is really going."

When Rocky was dying and the doctors couldn't find out why, who was there with him? I was. I walked with him through that terrible ordeal. The doctors did find out what he had in the nick of time. I told him he was just too mean to die. I'm grateful God spared Rocky. I need him.

Who was there for me when my wife, Sandy, and I had the worst year of our lives? Rocky was. The waves of trouble kept crashing against us: a divorce in the family, a close friend battling a serious illness, and leaving our church after seventeen years. It was a nightmare stretch. Rocky supported me through it all.

What Accountability Looks Like

Do what Rocky and I do. The centerpiece of our accountability relationship is our once-a-week, one-hour, face-to-face meetings. We use my office to insure total privacy. If one of us has to miss a meeting, he'd better have the world's best reason.

First, one at a time, we share what happened in our lives that week. We pay particular attention to our areas of weakness. We confess our sins. We tell the truth. This is not a general overview of the week. That's not accountability. That's a waste of time. This is a specific, under the microscope sharing of the gory details of a flawed man's week.

Second, we ask each other specific and probing questions about our areas of sin and weakness. We want to make sure we don't miss anything or cover anything up. My main problem is workaholism, so that's what Rocky zeroes in on. Here is the list of questions Rocky nails me with every week:

- How many hours did you work this week?

- When did you leave the office each evening?

- How long was your lunch break each day?

- Did you spend thirty minutes talking with Sandy each day?

- Did you pray with Sandy at least three times this week?

- Did you take Sandy out on a date this week?

- What specific time did you spend with each of your children this week?

- Did you ask Sandy every day what she needed from you?

- Did you ask Sandy at least once if she thinks you're working too hard?

- Did you have a quiet time each morning this week?

If this seems like the Spanish Inquisition, it is. Rocky could easily have been a prosecuting attorney. He asks these questions and expects truthful answers. I need this questioning to keep my workaholism at bay and enjoy quality time with my Lord, Sandy, and my four children. I have made a specific deal with Rocky about my weekly schedule. I know the right answers to all his questions. If I give the wrong answer, it won't be pretty.

I want to walk closely with Jesus. I want to maintain intimate, healthy relationships with my wife and kids. I don't want Satan to take me out of the game. I don't want to hurt those closest to me. Rocky, with these questions, keeps me on the right path.

Third, we pray for each other. We list our requests and then, one at a time, lift them up to God. Do you know what it's like to hear a dear friend pray for you in a direct, specific, and heartfelt way? It's humbling. It's intimate. It's convicting. It's motivating. I need it. Rocky needs it. You need it.

Fourth, we call each other during the week if necessary. If I'm really struggling and facing stress and temptation in my sin area, I call Rocky. We talk it out and pray together.

Find a trustworthy, devoted, believing accountability partner of the same sex in your community. Tell this person the total truth about your problem area. Meet face-to-face once a week in a private place. Share exactly what happened in your life the past week. Create a list of specific questions about your weakness for your partner to ask you. Pray together to end the meeting. Stay in contact by phone as needed.

Ask your partner to read this book and hold you accountable for doing the assignments in it. Discuss the Do Your Work section at the end of each chapter with your accountability partner. If you see a therapist, tell your partner about the sessions and the work you're doing.

If it takes a while to find a local accountability partner, it's okay to do it by phone with a trusted person who lives out of your area. This isn't ideal, but God will use it until you locate someone closer to home.

What If I Don't Have a Best Friend to be My Accountability Partner?

You may be thinking, *But I don't have a friend like Rocky right now.* That's okay. Don't worry. Although the closeness and mutuality (both of you sharing deeply and asking the tough questions) of a close friendship is ideal for accountability, it's not required. Use someone else for now. I believe God does have a best friend for you, so start praying for one and start looking. Until you find your best friend, you need to find someone else to hold you accountable.

Maybe the person you select will develop into a best friend, or at least become a good friend who will share personally and ask you to be a mutual accountability partner. Then again, maybe not. No big deal. It's perfectly okay and effective to have a one-way accountability relationship with a godly, good-hearted, mentor-type person. In this situation, your partner holds you accountable, but you don't hold your partner accountable.

Your accountability partner could be a friend. Your partner could be a leader in your church: pastor, elder, deacon, Bible-study leader, Sunday school teacher, small group leader. Your partner could be someone in your church, neighborhood, or place of employment whom you respect and trust. Your partner could be a family member: dad, mom, sister, brother, aunt, uncle, or cousin.

The person you choose must meet four critical requirements: be the same sex as you, know Jesus Christ personally and have a vibrant relationship with Him, keep your secrets and tell no one what you share, and be able to commit to an hour-long, face-to-face meeting each week and phone time as needed.

Your Local Church

The second essential team member is your local church. You must—I repeat, you *must*—be an active member of a local body of Christ. If you are a Christian, you need to be in church on a regular basis.

Quite a few Christians tell me they don't need to be in church. They say they can be good and effective Christians outside of a local body of Christ. They say they can worship and grow spiritually and serve God on their own. I give them two responses.

One, I tell them God wants them to be part of a local church. A large part of the New Testament is devoted to the founding and development of the church. The local church is God's chosen instrument to change the world—and the individuals in it. Do not drift away from the local church, but be a committed member (Hebrews 10:25; Acts 2:42; Ephesians 4:14–16).

Two, I ask them what trauma happened in church to drive them away. Almost every Christian not attending church has a story of how fellow Christians in a particular local body of

Christ caused deep hurt. This trauma must be worked through and healed. It becomes part of the recovery process.

If you are not a Christian yet, I still urge you to find a church. It's a great place to begin a relationship with Jesus and learn how to live life with His power and guidance.

To find a good church, ask a few Christians you respect to tell you about their churches. If you don't know any Christians, call Focus on the Family at 1-800-A-FAMILY and get a list of Christian therapists in your area. These therapists will be able to recommend some good churches.

What are the benefits of being involved in a local church? Too many to describe, but here's a brief list: worship, biblical knowledge, training in evangelism and discipleship, spiritual growth and maturity, conviction of sin, finding and using your spiritual gifts to serve others, support, encouragement, love, accountability, and close relationships.

It may be difficult to be in church. Maybe you've been mistreated by a church and some of the people in it. It's very likely that your relationship with God is strained because of your emotional pain. Push yourself to attend the worship service of a local church. Take it slowly. God wants you there. As you heal, you'll be able to branch out into relationships and areas of service.

Your One-Flesh Partner
If you are married, your spouse is a key member of your recovery support team. If you aren't married, skip to the next section. The two of you are one flesh (Genesis 2:24; Matthew 19:5), which means you are involved in the most deeply intimate and personal relationship on earth. You are to know each other inside and out. You are to be inseparable. United. The ultimate team.

Ideally, you go through the process of recovery and healing

together. Just as you share everything else with your one flesh partner, you and your spouse will share every step of your recovery. The support, love, and encouragement of your spouse are invaluable. The bond you forge along the way to emotional health will connect you on a deep level, possibly a level you have never known.

God wants you better. He also wants your marriage to be better. And much closer. Sharing the experience of recovery can accomplish both. At the end of the recovery journey, God wants you to be able to say, "I'm an emotionally healthy person, and I've never been closer to my spouse!"

In my therapy, I always seek to involve the client's spouse. I want the two of them to be a team. I see the couple in a joint session early on and explain how I want them to work together. I warn them that when one spouse changes, the marriage changes. I lay out my program of healing so the spouse knows exactly what will be happening. I urge my client to go home after each session and share, in detail, what work was done. Every insight, every step of progress, every painful memory, and every letter is shared with the spouse.

Urge your spouse to find a close friend of the same sex for support. A trusted confidant will give your mate the energy needed to help you through the healing journey.

An Uncooperative Spouse

If your spouse refuses to go through your recovery with you, you will still be able to heal completely. God will see to that. The other members of your support team become even more important. Unfortunately, without the involvement of your spouse, your marriage will not benefit from a shared healing experience. In fact, your relationship will be damaged by your spouse's disloyalty. When you are emotionally healthy, you can deal in an assertive way with your marital problems.

If your spouse isn't a Christian but *is* willing to help, let him or her assist you through your recovery. The two of you will become closer emotionally, and God may use your recovery journey to lead your spouse closer to Himself.

What Oneness Looks Like

You'll read this book and then your spouse will read it. You'll agree, and confirm it in prayer, to work together on all six steps in the recovery program. If your spouse is ready to work on his or her emotional problem, you will help each other heal at the same time. Or you could take turns: You go first, and then your spouse will go through the steps.

Discuss with your spouse the Do Your Work sections at the end of each chapter. You will tell your spouse the truth, in detail, about your emotional problem. You will use part of your daily, private, thirty-minute marriage-building talk time (you have one of these, don't you?) to share with your spouse your progress in recovery. You'll share your pain. Your emotions. Your thoughts. What you're learning. How you're changing. How your changes are affecting your marriage. What's happening with your accountability partner. Your relationship with God and how it's being transformed through your work. In other words, you share just about everything with your spouse as you battle your way through the steps of healing.

The one exception is for those who are struggling with sexual sin. You must tell your spouse when you act out sexually, but do not share the fantasies and temptations that come into your mind. These nasty thoughts will seriously erode your mate's security and do unnecessary damage to your relationship. Share these with God, your accountability partner, your twelve-step group (if you're in one), and your therapist (if you have one).

During every daily talk time, hold hands and pray specifically for God's help and healing. Ask Him for courage, strength, and motivation to do what you have to do. The power of prayer cannot be overestimated. Claim, over and over, the wonderful promise Jesus gave in Matthew 18:19: " 'Again I say to you, that if two of you agree on earth about anything that they may ask, it shall be done for them by My Father who is in heaven.' "

A Small Group

While not essential like the first two support team members, I urge you to join a small group. A small group is where you truly connect with others. It's where you get love, encouragement, real support, feedback, camaraderie, prayer, and strength for the journey of recovery. And we're all on the journey of recovery. It could be a home group. A Bible study. A men's group or a women's group. A twelve-step group. Just make sure it's a Christ-centered small group. We know who the higher power is. It's Jesus Christ. The power of a small group is nothing short of amazing. I've seen thousands of individuals change because of the influence of such a group.

God likes small groups. In fact, they were His idea in the first place. (He has all the good ideas!) The early church was composed almost entirely of small home groups. Jesus and His disciples were a small group. Paul talks about elders and deacons in the local church. These are small groups. Jesus promises to be present in every small group that meets together in His name (Matthew 18:20).

If you're battling an addiction to food, sex, alcohol, drugs, gambling, or codependency (among many possibilities), then a small group moves from a great option to an absolute essential. It will be extremely difficult to beat your addiction without the support and power of a twelve-step group.

I'm in a small men's group every Friday morning. Most of us attend the same church, and we call ourselves BOB: Band of Brothers. David, Rick, Rick, and Jesse. These are my guys. We study the Bible, share our lives, help one another find jobs when necessary, and pray for each other. These guys have changed my life.

A Christian Therapist

People usually assume that because I'm a Christian psychologist I think everyone ought to be seeing a therapist. I don't feel that way. A trained, licensed Christian therapist who is an expert in emotional problems and the recovery process may be an essential member of your team. But then again, maybe not.

I recommend you read this book and, together with your support team members, work through the steps of my healing strategy. I also urge you to use your pastor or a lay counselor at your church to help you follow the book's steps. That may be enough to get you well. But if you're still stuck and are not breaking through to emotional and spiritual health, find a Christian therapist.

If you live in an area without Christian therapists, then God will use members of your support team, your pastor, and possibly a lay counselor to heal you. He can do that because He's God.

If you live in an area where there are Christian therapists—and if you need one—find the best one. This is your emotional health we're talking about. You want a highly trained, experienced, licensed therapist who is a committed Christian—in fact, a Christian first, a therapist second. The therapist might be a doctoral-level psychologist or a master's-level mental health counselor or marriage and family therapist.

Ask your pastor and family doctor for names. Call Focus on the Family for a list of Christian therapists in your area. Call the therapists and get their credentials: Do they know Jesus? Do they attend a local church? Do they have a license? How many years have they been practicing? What is their basic approach to therapy and the recovery process? Look for someone who is active, directive, and gives homework assignments. A therapist who passively nods and occasionally asks, "How does that make you feel?" won't be much help.

Frankly, you want a therapist who will assertively direct you through the steps outlined in this book. Ask your therapist to read the book, and say this is the approach you want to follow. Every therapist has a different style and personality, but the steps of recovery are essentially the same.

All right. I've covered the human members on your support team. Start gathering them. In the next chapter, we'll talk about the supernatural member. He's the most important member of all. He's the one who does the healing.

Do Your Work

1. Who can you ask to be your accountability partner? What fears would keep you from asking? When will you ask? Write down the list of hard, specific questions that relate directly to your emotional problem you need your accountability partner to ask you.

2. If you don't attend church, what's stopping you? Discuss these obstacles with your accountability partner and spouse. If you do attend church, what's it like for you? Are you as involved as you can be? Could you get more involved?

3. Ask your spouse, if you have one, to be on your team as you work on your emotional problem. Pray as a couple that God will be with you as you go through the work together.

4. Are you in a small group? If not, do you think you could benefit from a small group? If so, what kind of a small group and where?

5. What are your thoughts about seeing a Christian therapist? What would stop you? Ask your accountability partner and spouse if they think you need to see a therapist.

CHAPTER 4

SMALL FAITH, BIG GOD:
HOW TO HEAL WHEN YOU'RE NOT CLOSE TO GOD

You can heal yourself. You don't need God or any other supernatural force. You don't even need other people. You can do it on your own. All you have to do is dig down deep and discover your own amazing power and wisdom. You've got what it takes inside to make it through anything and become an even stronger, smarter, and more incredible human being.

Where did I learn this? From reading celebrity profiles in popular magazines and newspapers. You've read these articles, haven't you? They're all the same. Certain celebrities speak candidly about how they emerged from painful, traumatic experiences with emotional and spiritual wholeness. They do often mention being positively influenced by others—family members, friends, therapists, spiritual gurus, children—but ultimately they give themselves the credit for their miraculous recoveries.

They admit it was tough for a while, but somehow they summoned the inner resilience and creative energy to turn disaster into triumph. Against all the odds, *they* did it. *They* healed themselves. *They* are special. They also have millions of dollars in the bank to cushion themselves from life's hardships.

They're full of baloney! These self-centered, clueless celebrities just don't get it. They haven't healed! They're worse off than they were before the pain hit. Instead of acknowledging and turning away from the sin and selfishness inside them, they revel in it and call it their inner strength. They've learned nothing. They haven't grown emotionally or spiritually an inch.

Their next disaster is right around the corner, and the story of their self-made recovery will be in all the same magazines and newspapers.

You can't heal yourself. And no other human person can heal you. There's only one Person who can truly heal you. His name is God, and He is the most important member of your recovery team.

God Is the Only One Who Heals

We read example after example in the Old Testament of the healing touch of God. Who healed King David of his shame and guilt? God did. Who healed Job? God did. Who healed Naaman the Syrian leper? God did. Who healed King Hezekiah? God did. I could go on and on. Everyone healed in the Old Testament was healed by God. God healed these individuals, and He'll heal you, too.

In the New Testament, Jesus Christ—in the power of God the Father—healed many people. Not only physically, but also emotionally and spiritually. When Jesus healed someone, it was a complete healing. In Luke 4:18 and John 8:36, we read the wonderful news that Jesus came to earth to free us from all the things that keep us in bondage. This includes our emotional problems.

I could quote a hundred verses—no, a thousand—that speak of God's healing power. Here are two:

The righteous cry, and the LORD hears and delivers them out of all their troubles. The LORD is near to the brokenhearted and saves those who are crushed in spirit (Psalm 34:17–18).

I can do all things through Him who strengthens me (Philippians 4:13).

God will hear you. He will deliver you. He will be near to you. He will save you. He will give you the strength to do your work and heal. These are promises God makes to you. He hasn't broken a promise yet.

Ezekiel 36:26 communicates another terrific promise: "I will give you a new heart and put a new spirit within you; and I will remove the heart of stone from your flesh and give you a heart of flesh." Now, that's what I'm talking about! If this isn't the world's best definition of healing, I don't know what is. God's going to give you a new heart and a new spirit. You're going to have to work for it, but God will power the process and provide a brand-new, healthy you.

The story of Nehemiah illustrates the roles you and God will play in the recovery journey. Nehemiah and his ragtag group of refugees faced many obstacles when rebuilding the wall around Jerusalem. Nehemiah relied on God and told the people repeatedly that God would protect them and give them success in their mammoth task. At the same time, Nehemiah put a specific plan into action. He told the people they would have to fight their enemies and work hard on the wall.

At one point, their enemies were threatening to sneak in and kill the workers. Nehemiah gathered together his people and delivered a message General George Patton would have envied: " 'Do not be afraid of them; remember the Lord who is great and awesome, and fight for your brothers, your sons, your daughters, your wives and your houses' " (Nehemiah 4:14).

That's the same message I'm delivering to you. God will do His job. He will heal you and give you that new heart and new spirit. You have to do your job, too. You've got to fight for your recovery. You've got to work hard to heal.

God Is the Point of the Pain

I'm a bottom-line guy, so here's the bottom-line reason you need to work through the pain of your emotional problem: to be closer to God and be a more effective servant for Him. Yes, God wants you to be emotionally healthy so you can experience the abundant life and great relationships with others. But ultimately God wants to be in an intimate relationship with you and to mold you into a sold-out spiritual warrior in His kingdom army.

You are not the point of the painful recovery process. *God* is the point. God allows pain in your life because He wants to move you closer to spiritual maturity and to Him. "We also exult in our tribulations, knowing that tribulation brings about perseverance; and perseverance, proven character; and proven character, hope; and hope does not disappoint, because the love of God has been poured out within our hearts through the Holy Spirit who was given to us" (Romans 5:3–5).

This is God's chain reaction of spiritual growth: tribulation, perseverance, proven character, hope, and finally the love of God poured out within our hearts. I want that last one, the love of God. Don't you? But I can't get the love of God without having my faith in God tested and built through the other brutal steps. It's the same for you.

It always takes tribulation and pain to get the job of faith building done. Always.

But I Have Zero Faith Now

"Doc, how can I even begin the recovery process when I have no faith right now? Why would God help me if I don't trust Him? I mean, I'm not close to Him at all. In fact, I'm doubting Him. I'm mad at Him." If these are your thoughts, you have good questions. I've heard them from thousands of clients as they start the steps of recovery.

You don't need a lot of faith in God to move through the healing process. In fact, next to zero faith in God is just fine. Perfectly normal. All you need is the tiniest bit of faith. Just enough to hang in there, and even though God seems far away and you don't feel good about Him, keep on slogging through the recovery steps.

Do you want to get a good look at some outstanding examples of weak, nearly nonexistent faith in God? I refer you again to the Hebrews 11 Hall of Famers. How could God enshrine these individuals in the Christian Faith Hall of Fame? A quick glance at the biographies of every member reveals shocking lapses of faith.

Take Abraham, the father of the Israelite nation. God made an unprecedented, sacred covenant with him. God blessed Abraham and revealed His holy presence and power to him on many occasions. What did Abraham do? Not just once but twice he lied and called his wife his sister in order to protect himself. He questioned and doubted God. He didn't trust God. Even though God told him He would give him a son, Abraham didn't believe Him.

Abraham was fearful. A coward. A liar. He threw his wife to the Egyptian wolves to save his own skin. At times, many times, his faith in God was weak. Pathetically weak. Even nonexistent. Sound familiar? I'm just like Abraham. You're just like Abraham.

But Abraham did have some faith. He's in the Hall, isn't he? He had enough faith to not quit. He had enough faith to keep coming back to God, even though he didn't feel like it. He had enough faith to do what God wanted him to do. Along the way, through all the ups and downs in his relationship with God, Abraham's pathetic faith grew and matured.

I want you to be like Abraham. Start the healing with whatever faith in God you have. No matter how small. No matter how weak. Just commit to doing the steps. That will be enough faith. It was enough for Abraham and the other members of the Hebrews 11 Hall of Fame. It'll be enough for you.

It's Going to Be a Struggle

It's okay to have a weak, barely breathing faith before and during the recovery road. It's also okay to struggle with God as you work on your emotional problem. Just about everyone does. The only exceptions are people who are faking it and a handful of incredibly spiritual individuals. I'm not one of these, and I doubt you are either. So, you're going to struggle.

God is sovereign. He created the universe. He created you. He's in control of everything and everyone (Job 38–41; Ephesians 1:11). Nothing happens outside of His knowledge and control. He knew you'd develop your emotional problem. He has allowed the painful events in your life to happen. So you're forced to deal with Him.

When I say *struggle,* I mean being angry with God, furious beyond words, deeply hurt and disappointed in Him, questioning Him. It's to doubt God, His promises, His love for you, His goodness, and at times, His existence. *Why have these things happened? Why to me? What are You up to? What are You doing? Why don't You answer my prayers? Why are You helping others but not me? Are You even there?*

It's a scary thing to struggle with God. It seems dangerous. It feels like betrayal. It feels wrong. But it's not dangerous or a betrayal or wrong. It must be done, or you won't change and your faith in God won't grow an inch.

Fellow Strugglers in the Bible

Just about every major biblical character had a massive struggle with God en route to emotional and spiritual wholeness. Here are a few: Noah, Abraham, Jacob, Moses, Job, Samuel, David, Elijah, Isaiah, Jeremiah, Daniel, Peter, and Paul. You're in pretty good company, right? This is a who's who of spiritual giants, but they didn't get to be giants without wrestling with their God.

Let's take a look at two on the list. David, in the beginning of psalm after psalm, battles with God. He's angry, he's hurt, he's doubting, he's questioning, he's venting, and he's screaming for God's help. By the end of each psalm, he has worked through his issues with God and is praising his heavenly Father. But he had to struggle first.

If anyone ever seemed to have a legitimate beef against God, it's Job. He was the most righteous man on earth (Job 1:8), but God allowed Satan to completely destroy his life. Job had a mighty struggle with God. God allowed him to thoroughly express his terrible emotional, physical, and spiritual agony. It was an integral part of Job's healing. Because Job faced God and was brutally honest, he was able to come back to God as recorded at the end of the book.

Keep in mind, David and Job did not become obsessed with their struggle with God. Neither did the other spiritual giants in the Bible. They struggled with God, but also did what He wanted them to do to heal. They got their recovery work done. That's what I want you to do.

Ethel and Ed: A Love Story

Ethel Harris is far more than a secretary to me. She's my right-hand woman, a godly, wise, kind, and loyal mentor. She handles my clients with care and respect. She provides valuable input in just about every area of my business and life. I tell her every few weeks that she cannot retire. When she's one hundred years old, we'll throw her a party. But then I want her back at her desk.

Most importantly, Ethel loves God and has a deep, mature

faith in Him. She has the inner spiritual beauty described in 1 Peter 3:4. For forty-eight years, she was married to a wonderful, sweet-spirited pastor named Ed. They served side by side in local church ministry for over sixteen years. They had a great marriage, were deeply in love, and raised four terrific daughters.

Several years ago, I witnessed Ethel's painful struggle to deal with the loss of her precious Ed. First came the stroke, and though Ed survived it for a time, he wasn't the same. One week later, Ed died, and a large part of Ethel's heart died with him.

Being a godly woman and close to God did not spare Ethel the terrible grief that overwhelmed her. She was devastated. Deeply hurt. Depressed. Sad. So very lonely.

Ed's death had come only six years after his retirement as a pastor. They were going to travel. Spend time together like they never could while in the ministry. See the grandkids often. Grow old together. All this was gone because Ed was gone.

Ethel's faith was severely tested. It was hard—impossible, really—to understand why God would allow this. Hadn't they served Him faithfully? Didn't they love Him? Didn't He care about them? How could God hurt her like this?

Ethel struggled with God as she tried to adjust to losing Ed. She was open and honest with her feelings and doubts and fears and grief. We had some deep, heart-wrenching talks as she slowly worked through the painful steps of recovery.

Ethel's not over it. You don't get over the loss of a beloved spouse, partner, and soul mate. But she is getting through it and moving forward. And because of her struggle with God, she's closer to Him than she's ever been.

Tear Faith Down to Build It Up

Just once I'd like to hear a testimony in church—in front of the entire congregation—from a Christian who is in the *middle* of the recovery process. Someone whose faith is currently weak. Someone struggling right now with God. Someone who shares honestly the fears, the doubts, and the difficulties of the recovery process. Someone who has not made it to emotional health and a closer relationship with God.

How ragged! How awkward! How unsettling! But oh, how beautiful that would be. Why? Because that's reality. What a breath of fresh spiritual air! The cleaned-up, sanitized testimonies often heard in church and in the Christian media—no matter how sincere—don't present the entire truth. When someone's faith has already been strengthened and they're looking back at what happened, the pain and misery just don't come across.

When you're right in the middle of the battle, it's ugly and messy, and faith is hard to come by. But that's exactly the way it's supposed to be. My faith, David's faith, Job's faith, Ethel's faith, and your faith will be torn down and then rebuilt during the process of recovery. Faith means hanging in there and struggling with God when you don't understand what He's doing.

One Way to God

I would love for you to know God as we embark on the recovery journey together. If you don't know God yet, now—right now—would be a great time to begin a relationship with Him. God provides the power to heal. Without Him, you can't get completely better. Human effort alone won't be enough. You must know God.

It's only through Jesus Christ that you can connect with God, get His power to heal and live a dynamic life here on earth, and go to heaven when you die.

There is only one God in the universe, the God described in the pages of the Bible. In 1 Corinthians 8:6, Paul wrote, "There is but one God, the Father, from whom are all things and we exist for Him." People who worship any god or religion other than the God of the Bible, no matter how sincere, are wasting their time.

There is only one way to reach the one true God, and that is through His Son, Jesus Christ. John writes these words spoken by Jesus: " 'I am the way, and the truth, and the life; no one comes to the Father but through Me' " (John 14:6).

God loves you and wants to have a personal relationship with you through Jesus. He loved you so much that He sent Jesus to die on a cross for all your sins—all the things you have done wrong in your life, and all the things you ever will do wrong until you die. Read John 3:16, God's message of love to you: " 'For God so loved the world, that He gave His only begotten Son, that whoever believes in Him shall not perish, but have eternal life.' "

If you want to know God and be a genuinely spiritual person, you must believe what 1 Corinthians 15:3–4 says about Jesus Christ: "I delivered to you as of first importance what I also received, that Christ died for our sins according to the Scriptures, and that He was buried, and that He was raised on the third day according to the Scriptures."

When you believe Jesus died on the cross for all your sins and was resurrected, and when you trust Him for forgiveness of your sins, you are a Christian. You know God. You have been made alive in Christ. You are spiritually alive. (For a fuller explanation of Christianity and the claims of Jesus Christ, please read *The Case for Christ* by Lee Strobel.)

You're Ready to Work
God loves you. He's crazy about you. If He sent His only Son to die for you, He won't stop there. He wants you to become emotionally healthy and to be closer to Him. He will not give up on you.

God is working a plan. He's understands your weak faith and your struggles. He wants you to deal with Him authentically. I hope you know God through Jesus as you begin your journey of healing. But if you do not, I pray you will meet Him along the way.

All right. It's time to begin work on your problem.

Do Your Work

1. Do you believe God has the power to heal you? Do you believe that God wants to heal you?

2. What is your faith in God like right now? How do you feel about God? Are you struggling with Him because of your emotional pain? Can you accept that this struggle is okay?

3. Are you willing to commit to persevering despite your weak faith and to follow the steps of recovery?

4. Think of a person you know who went through a trauma, wrestled with God, gutted it out through the pain, healed, and built a closer relationship with God through the process. Write out that person's story and read it as needed for encouragement. If you can, ask this person to pray for you as you take the steps of recovery.

5. Do you know God through His Son, Jesus Christ? Have you ever made this decision that affects all of life and eternity? If not, please talk to someone who is a Christian—your spouse, accountability partner, pastor, family member, or a small group member. Ask that person to explain about his or her relationship with God.

CHAPTER 5

CONFESSION IS GOOD FOR THE UNHEALTHY SOUL: AN AUTOBIOGRAPHY THAT BRINGS YOUR PROBLEM INTO THE LIGHT

My client took a seat on my couch for the first time and told me her story. She was a Christian woman in her thirties. Married to a good guy. A couple of kids. Actively involved in her church. Daily quiet times with God and participation in a weekly ladies' Bible study.

She looked down, paused, and then said, "My problem is that I'm depressed. I really don't know why, but in the last couple of years I feel myself slipping down deeper and deeper into a pool of sadness. I've never been a particularly happy person, but my depression is clearly getting worse. God's been good to me, and I have so many things to be thankful for. I ought to be happy, but I'm not. I find my life boring and predictable. I'm in a rut. I'm nowhere near the abundant, joyful life I think God wants me to have.

"I'm tired a lot of the time. I eat too much and can't get motivated to exercise. I don't like myself very much. I'm fat, unattractive, and can't do many things well. I lack confidence and seem to think negatively about everything. I have trouble speaking up with others and sharing what I genuinely think and feel. I'm afraid they won't be impressed with what I have to say.

"My close relationships aren't going too smoothly. I'm irritable and snappy with the kids. I lose my temper with them too often, and I feel terrible afterwards. I want to enjoy my precious children, but they're driving me crazy.

"I love my husband, and I know he loves me. But I can't give myself to him fully—emotionally, spiritually, or sexually. I don't trust him with my personal thoughts and feelings. I can't open up and share my heart honestly with him. I can't share my needs with him. I can't tell him when he hurts me. It seems risky to communicate the truth to him. For some reason, I'm scared he'll end up rejecting me.

"I'm not close to God, either. I desperately want an intimate relationship with Him, and I've tried for years to develop one. Prayer, Bible study, service in the church, longer quiet times, weekend spiritual retreats. You name it; I've tried it. But nothing has worked. I don't trust God totally. I don't feel like I can truly please Him. I'm just not good enough for Him. I can't seem to give Him complete control of my life."

After taking a thorough history of her life and her depression, I had a good understanding of her problem. The trouble was, *she* didn't. She knew she was depressed and miserable. But that was about it.

I asked her why she was depressed. She didn't know. I asked her to tell me the possible sources of her depression. She didn't know. I asked her what incorrect, irrational thoughts were fueling her depression. She didn't know. I asked her what service her depression was providing her. What were the payoffs for being depressed? She didn't know.

Her depression was a monster that was ruining her life. It was sucking her dry of all energy and passion. It was crippling all her relationships. But she didn't know anything about it.

She asked me, "Should I know more about my depression than I do?"

I answered, "No, not right now. All the clients I've seen have had next to zero insight into their problems. But we're going to change that. To break the grip of a problem, you must get to know it intimately. You must find out how it operates. The power of a problem largely comes from its mystery and secrecy. We're going to drag your problem out of the darkness and into the light. We're going to completely expose it."

The Story of Your Life

This lady's first assignment in the school of Dave Clarke therapy was to write her autobiography—the story of her life and her depression. I wanted all her background information: her mom and dad; her siblings; what it was like growing up in her home; how she was treated by her parents; the kind of relationships she had with grandparents and other extended family members; her school years; significant relationships with friends and the opposite sex; her relationship with God; traumatic experiences, abuse, or mistreatment by others; and what her marriage and family had been like to that point.

I asked her to weave in the story of her depression as she wrote her autobiography. As with most problems, her depression had its roots way back in her history. Her depression grew up and developed right along with her. I wanted her to write when she first felt depressed and why, to describe the times she felt more depressed than usual, how she coped with the depression, and who else knew about it. I asked her to pay particular attention to painful events in the past and how they connected to her depression and to cover what the last few years of deepening depression had been like.

She commented, "This is going to be very difficult."

I said, "You're right, it will be. But it's an important step in your recovery."

Then she asked, "Why do I have to do this?"

I replied, "I'm glad you asked. I have my reasons."

Why Expose the Problem?

Writing out how your life and problem developed will help you find out how your problem operates. You'll find out how and when your problem started, the unresolved pain that first gave it life and still fuels it, the ways it has disrupted your expression of emotions, the lies that sustain it, the payoffs it provides, and what it has cost you.

Writing your autobiography helps you get at the truth. Telling the truth is a principle and command found throughout the Bible. In Ephesians 4:14–25 and Colossians 3:8–11, we read that telling the truth is a critical part of renewing our minds and becoming more like Jesus Christ.

Writing your autobiography brings your problem from darkness into light. Jesus is light, and He wants us to walk in the light, too (1 John 1:7; John 8:12).

Writing your autobiography gives you a forum to confess your sins (1 John 1:9). The Bible instructs us to confess directly to each other (Matthew 5:23–24; James 5:16). The Bible supports going into detail describing sinful behavior. The story of David's sin with Bathsheba (2 Samuel 11–12) and his confession of that sin (Psalm 51) is told in excruciating detail. Although not all emotional problems are sinful, most of them can lead to sinful behavior.

Writing your autobiography produces godly sorrow, the painful reaction of a person who understands the damaging impact of his or her behavior on others and on God. This kind of sorrow means being broken and humbled. Second Corinthians 7:9–11 teaches this progression: godly sorrow leads to repentance, which leads to changed behavior. What Paul is talking about in this passage is genuine heart change.

Writing your autobiography creates a crisis, and no one—no one—ever changes without a crisis.

Writing your autobiography makes what has happened in your life more real to you. It becomes more personal. It becomes more intense. You reach a much deeper level of emotional understanding and insight. Talking out the history of your problem, important as that is, isn't good enough. When you write it out, there's nowhere for you to hide. Denial and rationalization and ignorance are swept away by the cold, hard facts on paper. You force yourself to see everything.

Finally, writing your autobiography helps you grieve your sin (James 4:6–10). You'll hate your unhealthy behavior. You'll loathe it. And that's what you need to do to be motivated to defeat it and start living a new life.

One Woman's Story

I took a few minutes to pray with my depressed client. I asked God to guide her through the assignment and reveal what He wanted her to write. We put God in charge of exposing the details of her problem and its growth to this point in her life. I asked her to pray this same prayer with her spouse, accountability partner, and pastor.

It took her four drafts to dig up the details. This is her final version, reduced to include only the parts of her history that clearly expose the sources and operation of her depression:

I'd have to say I had a pretty decent childhood. Not great, but pretty good. I mean, I knew kids who had it a lot worse than me. We were middle-class, had a nice home, my mom and dad stayed married, and we went to church regularly.

I had a good mom. She and I were close when I was young. She loved me and did many things for me. I spent quite a bit of time with her.

My dad loved me, I guess. We didn't have much time

together. The way my family worked was along gender lines: dad and my brother, Mike; mom and me. My dad clearly favored Mike and even though I wanted more time with Dad, it didn't happen.

Dad didn't understand me. I couldn't please him, no matter how hard I tried. Grades, chores, my appearance—it was never good enough. He was critical of me and gave out compliments about twice a year. He didn't say "I love you" and wasn't known for being affectionate.

The truth is, he was cranky and difficult to be around. Mom said he had a tough childhood, was stressed at his job, and didn't know how to relate to a girl. Oh well, that was the way it was. I'm sure I wasn't the only girl with a dad like that.

Oh, there was one thing that really did bother me. One day—I think I was almost out of elementary school—I accidentally came across my dad's box of pornography in the attic. I was shocked and repulsed by those filthy magazines. That did hurt me. I remember crying in my room for a long time. I never told a soul.

I want to discuss how my family handled the expression of emotions and opinions. From early on in my home—as far back as I can remember—emotions were not expressed. Dad could get angry, but no one else could. Dad—and Mom, too—just didn't let loose with their emotions. Everything was held in, stuffed down, and tightly controlled. Mike and I learned to squelch our feelings because we got punished for sharing anger, hurt, disappointment, or any other intense emotion.

I remember getting angry once when I felt Mike got special treatment from Dad. I actually said something at the table, and my dad told me, "Shut up. You have no right to feel that way." He told me in a loud voice (again, he *could* be angry) that I should be grateful to be in this family and to count my blessings.

It was the same way with any opinion I had. Once I entered middle school, I had some pretty strong opinions but was cut off at home when I tried to share them. If Dad didn't agree with my opinion (and he seldom did), he'd say something like, "Pipe down. You're wrong. What do you know about it?" He belittled me, so I stopped speaking up. He was always right, and I was always wrong. Period.

Mom and Dad didn't deal with conflict, at least, not that I ever saw. I really never saw them fight or work through a disagreement. I think Dad called the shots, and Mom didn't buck him. She kept the peace. I never knew how she felt about things or what her opinions were. She just kept on smiling and taking care of the home and us kids. She didn't work outside the home, although I think she wanted to. One day, she let it slip that she had dreamed of being an art teacher. When I probed, she just sighed and said, "Your father and I decided I should stay home with the kids." I figured it was Dad's decision, not hers.

I almost didn't write this, but I decided it was important. When I was around nine or ten, a neighbor friend's older brother fondled me. He was in high school. It was at a sleepover, and he came into the room where I was sleeping. I think he thought I was asleep. He pulled down my panties and rubbed me for a few minutes. There was a noise somewhere in the house, so he quickly left. It only happened that one time. I felt dirty, ashamed, and confused. I never told anyone.

As I'm writing this, I'm starting to realize my childhood was painful. Not horrible, but painful. I'm feeling sad now. Sad about my dad, sad about not being able to express my *emotions and opinions, and sad about being abused. Sad is a good word to describe most of my life.*

Middle school was bad. Bad. Bad. Bad. I think this is when I first felt depressed. I felt so stupid and awkward. Very self-conscious. I hated my nose and my long neck. Some of the boys called me giraffe. That really hurt, but I had to pretend it didn't. I wasn't that good in school. I wasn't that good in sports. I wasn't good-looking or popular. I wasn't much of anything. I didn't know who I was. I couldn't find something I was good at.

I played the clarinet but wasn't very good. My parents didn't push me to get involved in any activities. I didn't click in my church youth group. I had a few friends, but we didn't spend much time together. I spent a lot of time in my room.

One incident in middle school stands out. It was in eighth grade, and Mary, the most popular girl in school, was having a big party at her house. Everybody was talking about it. Everybody, even the few friends I had, seemed to be going. Except me. I didn't get an invitation. I thought I'd die from grief and sadness.

High school didn't get much better. I stayed depressed and apathetic most of the time. As I think back, I can see how the depression was limiting my life. I pulled inward. I lost all confidence and took no risks. I didn't try out for cheerleading or any sports. I didn't join any clubs. I didn't share my opinions, for fear I'd be rejected. I had a small circle of friends but didn't do many fun things. No boys asked me out. I did get better grades in high school, but that didn't make me feel any better about myself.

College was better—at first. I wanted to get a fresh start away from home. I made some good friends but still didn't have the guts to branch out and try new activities. I studied too much and should have had more fun. I did feel closer to God my freshman year. I was having regular quiet times, talking with Him more during the day, and attending a local church. I was developing my own faith and not just following what my parents believed.

Then I met David and everything changed. I met him at the beginning of my sophomore year, and we got serious right away. We dated all that year and were inseparable. I loved him and believed he loved me. I felt more alive and confident than I had in my whole life. My depression lifted, and the feeling was wonderful.

Right at the end of the year, we went all the way physically. I didn't plan to have intercourse, but it happened. I was so stupid. We had intercourse three more times. I will never ever forget staring at the home pregnancy test that told me I had a baby inside. I was horrified and scared out of my mind. And I felt terribly guilty. What was I going to do?

When I told David, his reaction killed me. He was confused. He was angry at me. He blamed me for not using protection. He convinced me I had to get an abortion. He took me to a clinic, paid for it, and I had the procedure. Two days later, he dumped me.

I was never the same after that. All my newfound confidence and self-esteem evaporated overnight, and I was as depressed as I'd ever been. I went home for the summer and told no one. I was too ashamed. I got through my last two years of college, but it was a blur.

I met my husband near the end of our senior year, and we fell in love. I told him about the abortion, and to my great relief, he didn't get upset. He just wanted me to be okay with it. We didn't talk much about it. I have moved on, and God has blessed me with my kids. But I still feel guilty about it.

The first few years of marriage were good, and my depression seemed better—not gone, but less intense and at least manageable. The kids came along, and I was too busy with them to really notice how I was feeling about myself and my life.

I still live my life in a safe, careful way. I don't take risks. I don't express my feelings too well. I don't do anything outside my comfort zone. I'm in a rut.

These last two years, I notice my depression is deepening. It's like I can't control it anymore. It's getting worse by the month, and I'm scared. I'm not happy except once in a while. And it never lasts long. I'm edgy, tired all the time, cynical, having outbursts of temper at the kids, not close to my husband, not close to my friends, and not close to God.

It doesn't take much to get me angry or to send me into a depressed funk: the kids being noisy or disobedient, my husband coming home late from work, having a disagreement with my husband, hearing a sermon about the victorious Christian life, talking with my parents on the phone. It could be anything that triggers me. My tolerance is shot.

I'm tired of being depressed. I want to be happy. I can see now how long I've been depressed and that depresses me. Maybe I'm just meant to be depressed my whole life. I hope not, but I don't know how to stop it.

My dad, that slimeball brother of my friend, and David all hurt me badly. I'm feeling angry at them but don't know what to do about it.

Study Your Story

Most of us have had English literature classes in which we had to read a short story or novel and then analyze it to death. The teacher makes the students comb through the story to discover the plot lines, the major themes, and all the symbolism the author had hidden in it. This is how English teachers make a living.

I remember one particular day in a literature class in college. The teacher spent an hour droning on about all the multiple meanings of rain in one author's story. I wanted to stand up and scream, "Stop it! You cannot be serious! I don't mind a little symbolism, but this is ridiculous. If this author could walk in here right now, he'd laugh his head off. He'd tell us that he just wrote a nice story to entertain people, and when it rained, all it meant was that it was raining."

Even though this isn't an English lit class, I want you to carefully study the story you've written. This examination will be meaningful and beneficial to you.

First, read your story out loud to God and ask Him to help you gain insight into your problem. Next, read it yourself three times and write down your answers to these questions:

1. How did your home life contribute to your problem?

2. When did your problem begin to develop?

3. How did it develop over the years?

4. How did you learn to express your emotions?

5. How did you learn to express your thoughts and opinions?

6. What are the major painful events in your life?

7. How have these events fed your problem?

8. Have you faced and worked through these events?

9. Who has significantly hurt you in your life?

10. Whom have you significantly hurt?

11. What incorrect, irrational, and unhealthy thoughts do you believe about yourself and the world around you?

12. Who taught you these lies?

Second, read your story and your answers to the above questions to members of your support team. Read out loud to each person in a private place and ask for specific feedback with questions like these:

- What are your impressions of my story?

- Do you think I left out any major painful events?

- What input can you give on how my problem has developed over the years?

- What would you add to or change about my answers to the questions?

Of course, each team member will also provide support and empathy as you read your story.

The Road Map to Recovery

The written story, the readings, and the answered questions lay a foundation for the work of recovery. Your story is a road map that shows where you have to go and what you have to do to heal.

My depressed client's story shows how her problem

developed and what she'll have to do to fix it. Her depression began with her dad's mistreatment and her parents teaching her to stuff her emotions and opinions. The incorrect, negative thoughts—the lies she told herself—also began in her home: I'm not worthy, I'm not smart, I'm not pretty, I must stuff my emotions, and so on. The sexual abuse at her friend's house was a huge factor in her developing depression.

She came into middle school already depressed and with low self-esteem. These brutal years solidified her depression and gave it deep roots. Her lies about herself became set in concrete. The breakup with her college boyfriend and the abortion further deepened her depression.

Marriage and children distracted her for a while, but her depression—which was always there—has roared back to life. She can't manage her depression anymore, and it's getting worse. Her unresolved relationship with her dad and the depression itself block her from close, healthy relationships with her husband and God. She has a safe, limited, and increasingly depressed life. She has learned how to keep herself depressed, and she does that every single day of her life.

The elements of her healing process are all in her story. She has to identify her lies and learn to attack them and replace them with the truth. God's truth. She has to learn to express her emotions and opinions. She has to deal directly with those who harmed her in the past. She has to deal directly with those she harmed. She has to forgive others and herself. She has to connect with God on a deeper level. She has to build a new life in which she can live out God's adventure for her.

She's going to be able to take all the steps in the recovery process, one at a time. So will you.

Do Your Work

1. Write the autobiography of your life and your problem. Pray that God will bring up the details and pain you need to remember. Write two or three drafts if necessary.

2. Read your story to God and pray for insight. Read it three times to yourself and write down your answers to the twelve questions listed earlier in this chapter.

3. Read your story and your answers to the questions out loud to members of your support team. Ask each for input.

4. How much do you hate your problem? Are you in godly sorrow over your unhealthy behavior? How badly do you want to get better? Give your answers to these questions to the members of your support team, and ask them if they think you're ready to do your recovery work.

CHAPTER 6

NO MOTIVATION, NO CHANGE: HOW BADLY DO YOU WANT TO GET BETTER?

I like to honk my car horn. Frequently. I consider my horn to be the most important tool in my driving arsenal. Because I'm such an excellent driver, it's my civic and automotive duty to use my horn to keep the roadways safe and efficient. I use my trusty horn to express my feelings, to protect myself, to protect others, to keep traffic moving, and to teach other drivers basic skills they do not possess.

I can't tell you how many times other motorists have pulled me over to thank me for honking my horn. They usually say something like, "I don't know who you are, but I want to thank you for giving me the horn back there. That took guts. I know you didn't enjoy it, but it had to be done. I was mad at first, but now I can see you were doing it for my own good. What I did was wrong and dangerous. Thanks to you, I learned something. Please, keep up the good work."

All right, that's never happened. I have gotten plenty of reactions to my honking, but I can't describe them in a Christian book. Despite the shocking lack of appreciation, I continue to be a frequent horn user.

Over the years, I have developed a variety of specific honks. I have a honk for virtually every driving situation. Here's a brief list:

The honk of outrage
A motorist makes a reckless move that endangers my life. This is the longest honk of all—a minimum ten-second blast.

The honk of despair
I'm caught in gridlock. It's no one's fault; I'm just venting with my horn.

The honk of triumph
I make five or six lights in a row on a brutal stretch of roadway where I usually rot at every miserable, long light. Or I perform some spectacular driving maneuver!

The honk of fear
I'm trying to avoid an accident. A motorist is about to hit my car. Often followed immediately by the honk of outrage.

The honk of appreciation
Another motorist makes an impressive driving action. This honk is often misunderstood.

The honk of instruction
A fellow motorist makes a mistake. A gentle but firm rebuke.

The honk of frustration
I'm late, and traffic is moving slowly. A simple release of tension. The honk of despair could follow.

The honk of happiness
I make a light I hardly ever make, and I'm exultant.

The honk of disgust
I see a motorist endanger the life and vehicle of another motorist. I'm safe, but I want the offending motorist to know that I saw what happened. I also use it on a motorist who impedes my progress for no good reason.

The honk of sympathy

Two short taps to communicate *that's a bummer* to a stranded motorist. This is also often misunderstood.

There are three types of individuals I highly recommend not honking at: a rookie in a driver's education vehicle, anyone on a Harley, and a motorist with a gun rack.

The Honk of Motivation

While these horns are all helpful, the most important honk of all is the honk of motivation. Why? Because this honk is used to address my biggest pet peeve on the road: the left-turn-lane wimp. This is the person who is first in the left-turn lane when the light is green, but who will not push out and turn left on the yellow. This person will not budge an inch unless there are no cars coming in the opposite direction for at least a mile.

This driver stays put as the light turns red. He will wait out an entire light cycle for the green arrow because that's when he feels safe to turn in front of the stopped line of traffic. If there is no green arrow, he will wait through three or four light cycles until he feels he has enough space to turn. He forces the entire line of cars behind him to wait because he's a wimp.

When I'm right behind a left-turn-lane wimp, I've got to do something to get him moving into the intersection. If I don't act, I'll have to languish at that light until my car runs out of gas. And so will all the drivers behind me. I take this heavy responsibility seriously.

To create a crisis and motivate the wimp to move, I use the honk of motivation. I blast my horn in short, staccato bursts. Sometimes, it works, and the person will actually push out and turn on the yellow light. If this happens, I sound the honk of appreciation as we both make the turn.

Most of the time, it doesn't work, and the person will not move. He deserves the honk of disgust, and that's what he gets.

Every now and then, I'm able to execute what I call the left turn of sweet victory. This is when I pull around the wimp and make the left turn on the yellow, leaving him in my dust. As he watches my tailgate disappear around the corner, he hears the honk of triumph. And he thinks, *That man can drive. I wish I could turn on the yellow.*

A driver holding up traffic is like a person who won't move forward and do the work of recovery. He can do it, but he refuses. He has the opportunity, but he won't seize it. He stays where he is.

The stakes are a lot higher for the person deciding whether to follow my recovery steps, but the principle is the same. If you're not motivated, you won't do the hard work of healing. Consider this chapter to be your horn of motivation.

Godly Sorrow as Motivation

As we saw in the last chapter, godly sorrow is necessary for genuine change. When you experience godly sorrow, you're grieving your sin and hating it the way God does. It makes you motivated to do anything to change your behavior. You can't get to godly sorrow without a crisis. The crisis is seeing clearly the terrible price your emotional problem is costing you and others close to you.

My depressed client had completed her autobiography assignment. She'd answered the twelve questions and received feedback from her support team members. She had a basic grasp of how her problem had developed over the years. But there was something else she needed before she was ready to tackle the rest of the recovery steps—genuine, godly sorrow and the motivation that comes from it. I told her that if she didn't have enough motivation, she'd never make it through my recovery program.

She asked me, "How can I find out if I have enough motivation?"

I replied, as I have to thousands of clients, "You have to realize the terrible cost of your problem."

Every Problem Has Its Payoffs

I asked my client to go home and, without talking to anyone, write a list of her depression's payoffs. She wanted to know what I meant by *payoffs*.

I told her every emotional problem provides special services. It's sort of like the benefits you get as an employee or by owning an insurance policy. "In other words," I asked, "what do you get out of being depressed? What does being depressed do for you?"

She was aghast and agitated. Insulted even. She told me she couldn't believe I was talking this way. "Why, my depression isn't doing anything for me. It's making me miserable and ruining my life!"

I replied, "I know it's causing you a lot of pain. But you're getting some things out of it, too. It's helping you avoid behavior you don't want to do."

With that little hint, I sent her home angry and annoyed with me. I asked her to pray that God would open her eyes to the payoffs and to jot them down for our next session.

She came back with a new attitude and new insight into her depression. She told me that God had shown her some truths she didn't want to see. She read me this list of payoffs:

- *My depression is an excuse for not being a better Christian, a better wife, a better mom, and a better friend.*

- *It keeps me from doing things I don't want to do or am scared to do. All I have to say or think to myself is, "I can't do that because I'm depressed."*

- *It's my excuse for yelling at the kids.*

- *It's my excuse for avoiding sex with my husband.*

- *It's my excuse for not regularly attending the women's Bible study at church.*

- *It's my excuse for not speaking up when someone angers me or hurts my feelings.*

- *It's my excuse for eating more than I should and not exercising.*

- *It's my excuse for not facing and dealing with my dad, my friend's brother, my college boyfriend, and the abortion. I think I've preferred being depressed to feeling the pain connected to these memories.*

She had developed a good list. It showed how she was hiding behind her depression to escape living the life God wanted her to live. She could keep choosing to use her depression in these ways forever or she could take the tough steps necessary to kill her depression and live a new life. It was up to her.

I sent her home to read her payoff list to her husband and her accountability partner and to get their feedback. She reported to me that these support team members had agreed with her list and even added a few more payoffs.

She made this insightful comment to me: "These aren't actually payoffs. They're part of the cost of my stupid depression, aren't they?"

"Bingo. You're absolutely right," I responded. "They just seem to be payoffs, but they're not. Your depression is denying you experiences that would enrich your life and make you a happy, healthy person."

It was time to get more aggressive with my depressed client. She needed to realize what her problem was costing her. I wanted her to be so nauseated and disgusted with her depression that she would do anything—anything—to be free of its life-sucking power.

To accomplish this goal, four letters had to be written. The first letter was to be written by her. I asked her to write out, in a letter addressed to herself, the high price of her depression. What it had cost her in the past. What it was costing her in the present. What it would cost her in the future. I wanted specifics and details, not generalities and broad statements. I told her if it was skimpy and too general, she'd do it again.

I asked her to pray that God would show her the true cost of her depression. I instructed her to ask her spouse and accountability partner to pray with her that she would do a good, thorough job on this assignment.

The other three letters were written by her accountability partner (who, in this case, is her close friend), her pastor, and her husband. I told her to ask these three supporters to write letters to her describing what they believed her depression was costing her and them. Her job was to urge them—beg if needed—to be brutally honest in their letters. They were not to spare her feelings or sugarcoat the truth in any way. Her emotional and spiritual health was at stake, and she had to have the absolute truth.

My plan was for her to do her letter in private and then wait for the other three to complete their letters. One by one—or in a group meeting if that could be arranged—the support team members would then read their letters out loud to her. Finally, she would read to them the letter she had written to herself.

Here are the four letters:

The Personal Letter

My job is to write what my depression has cost me—in the past, in the present, and in the future. I don't think I know the total cost, but I'll do my best.

As I reread my autobiography, I can see how much my depression cost me in the past. It cost me my self-esteem. I've always felt ugly and worthless. The pain my dad, my abuser, and David inflicted on me caused me to hate myself, and that self-hatred became part of my depression. I hated myself all the way through college. I spent hours and hours and hours—too many to count—crying in my room because I hated myself and my life.

Every disappointment seemed to crush me and further convince me of my stupidity and worthlessness. My depression made every painful event even worse in my mind. I can remember crying in my room for hours when I realized I was not invited to Miss Stuck-Up Mary's party. And I cried in my room for hours the evening of the party.

That's my main picture of my childhood: crying in my room. My depression made me a miserable prisoner in that room. I hate that room. I'd like to go back home and set fire to it. Or better yet, rent a bulldozer and flatten it to the ground.

The world kept going outside, but I was crying in my room. My depression robbed me of my childhood and adolescence. I want them back, but it's too late.

I think of the many opportunities in the past I wasted because I was depressed. Feeling sad and insecure kept me from doing so many things. Things that would have made me happier and helped me grow as a person. Things that would have gotten me out of that stupid, stinking room. Cheerleading. Sports. The Spanish club. Youth group activities and retreats. The hiking club. The Wednesday night dorm Bible study in college. The winter ski trip my junior year of college. I didn't do any of them thanks to my wretched depression. I just turned inward and nursed my many hurts and resentments.

In the present, it's the same story. My depression is robbing me of a full, vibrant life. Now I'm crying in my adult bedroom. I've just switched houses! I'm still focused on myself and my misery. I'm not that close to anyone. All my relationships could be better. A lot better. I don't seem to have the energy and the motivation to branch out and give myself to others. It suddenly dawns on me how selfish my depression has made me. It's all about me and trying to protect myself from getting hurt. The truth is that I am continuing to hurt myself by hiding behind my depression.

The list of activities I am avoiding goes on and on. Attending the women's Bible study every week. Getting involved with the middle-schoolers at church. Leading a Bible study in my neighborhood. Playing tennis Thursday mornings with Karen, Lisa, and Betty. Taking a psychology class at the university. I'm sick of living this barren existence! If I die today, just put on my tombstone: SHE WAS DEPRESSED AND CRIED IN HER ROOM.

The worst price my depression costs me today is my mediocre relationships with those I love the most. I don't have the energy or the tolerance I need to build closeness with my children. Instead of enjoying them and creating great memories, I get angry at them and distance myself. I'm cheating me and them. Just yesterday, my daughter asked me to look through a fashion magazine with her. I was having a bad day so I told her maybe another time. She's going to grow up, and I will have run out of times. I'm always having bad days. My whole life has been one never-ending bad day! It's time to have good days, at least most of the time.

My depression is squeezing the life out of my marriage. We're stable. We're okay. But we're not close. I feel unhappy so much that I don't strive to meet his needs. I can't seem to open up and really share myself with him. Sex is more of a chore than a joyful, passionate experience. I want a better marriage, but my depression is in the way.

My most precious relationship of all—with God—isn't going well. I keep God at a distance, too. I don't feel any spiritual vitality.

As for the future, all I can see, if I don't change, is more of the same. A restricted life. Wasted opportunities. Mediocre to poor relationships. Crying in my room. Whining about how bad my life is. Hating myself. Staying stuck in this miserable cycle of depression and self-loathing. Never becoming who God wants me to be. Never accomplishing what He wants me to accomplish.

Well, I'm sick to death of this depressed life. I want out of my room. Out of my prison. I'm keeping myself locked in there! I'm ready to do what I have to do to get out. I want to live! Really live!

The Accountability Partner Letter

I'm reluctant to write this letter because I want to be your supporter and encourager. But I guess this is part of supporting and encouraging. You've assured me that what

I write here will not push you away from me. I'm holding you to that promise. I love you and want you to get better. I hope and pray this truth from my viewpoint will help in your healing.

You are beautiful. You are smart. You have a quirky sense of humor when you lighten up and show it. You are kind and generous. You're a good mom. All these things are true. As your close friend, I should know. It's too bad you don't believe any of these qualities are true about you.

It just kills me to see and hear you be so down on yourself. You do it all the time. You criticize yourself constantly. I've often wondered why you are so hard on yourself. Nothing you do is ever good enough. You don't receive compliments well because you don't believe them. The other day, I commented on how pretty you looked in that green dress. You said, "Oh, this isn't quite in style anymore, and it shows too much of my stomach." One more compliment shot down in flames.

You won't get involved in activities that would be so good for you. You always seem to have an excuse. I know you'd enjoy the ladies' Bible study if you came every week. Coming sporadically keeps you from building closer relationships with the other ladies. Maybe that's why you don't come more often. I think you're scared of getting close. It's like you're afraid someone will hurt you like others have hurt you in the past.

Even though you have gifts and talents from the Lord, you find excuses not to use them. This may shock you, but I believe you have the gift of teaching. I can see you leading a small group and teaching the Bible. You know the Bible and can communicate its principles clearly. Why don't you? Because you're depressed.

You don't feel confident in your abilities. You're too tired. You wouldn't be good enough. I can just hear your excuses because I've heard them before.

Please forgive me for being blunt, but baloney! You can do it, and I pray one day you will.

I treasure our friendship, and I will love you whether you stay depressed or not. I just know if you heal from your depression, we'll be even closer. We'll be able to do more things together. We'll be able to laugh more, talk more deeply, and grow closer in the Lord.

Plus, I'll be a happier person. Your depression does affect me. I've never told you about this because I didn't want to hurt you, but I guess now's the time. Seeing you so unhappy makes me unhappy. I grieve over you often. I can't tell you how many times I've cried about you and the pain you're in. I spend hours praying that somehow God will heal you.

I've been angry with you, too. Angry that you cheat yourself out of a better life. A life God wants for you. When you backed out of the ladies' retreat last year at the last minute, I was furious with you. I should have told you so then. We were going to room together! It would have been a blast! Your lame excuse of not feeling well and having to catch up on housework made me mad. And then sad. Sad for you. Sad for me.

I want you to get better. It would be a burden lifted off of me, and we'd be much closer, but it's mainly for you. I want you to be happy and healthy. Please do whatever you have to do to get better. Too much time has gone by. Do it now.

The Pastor Letter

I've known you for eight years, and I love you, your husband, and children. I appreciate the several talks we've had and the pain you have shared with me.

That took courage to do. I don't know much about your past, but you have shared how miserable your depression is making you in the present. I have prayed for you and continue to pray for you. I thought it might be a good idea to put down on paper the things I've prayed:

Dear Father, I lift up this woman who is battling depression. It saddens me and You, Father, to watch one of Your children be so crippled by this problem. She has Your power but cannot seem to tap it. She has the opportunity to live an abundant life, but she's nowhere near it.

Father, You've given her some special spiritual gifts. She has a heart for middle-schoolers, maybe because of her own painful middle school years. She has told me she feels called to work with middle-schoolers at the church. I know she also has the gift of teaching. But she won't do it.

This depression is holding her back from this important ministry. I don't have people lining up to work with the middle school ministry. Father, You know that. I need her to do it. The church body needs her to do it. She needs to do it. Those kids need her to do it. Please remove the obstacles that are in the way.

Father, I pray that You will help this woman heal from her depression. I believe You want her to be healthy so she can be everything You want her to be. She is missing out on all the wonderful things You want her to have, especially and most importantly in her relationship with You. Help her heal, Father, so she can walk with You in intimate fellowship.

The Spouse Letter

Honey, I'm not much of a writer, but you asked me to write this, and I love you, so I'll give it a try. I don't want to hurt you. I want to help you get better. Please remember that as you hear these words.

I know you've always fought depression. You've had good days and even good months during our marriage. But these last few years have mostly been down ones for you. I hate to see you depressed and unhappy. It breaks my heart, over and over, to watch you criticize yourself and not do things I know you can do. You are so hard on yourself, and I can't convince you that you're wrong when you believe things that aren't true.

When we got married, I thought everything would be great. And it was—for a while. But your depression came back and hasn't left. I wanted to be the man who helped you heal from your dad's mistreatment and that dirtball who sexually abused you and David who burned you so badly in college. But, honey, you won't let me help you. I know I can't make it all better, but I could make a difference. You keep me at arm's length. You won't open up and talk to me. I can tell when you're stuffing your emotions, but when I ask you to talk, you won't do it. Do you know how frustrating that is for me? And then I have to watch you get snappy, irritable, and eventually blow up over some small thing a few days later.

Why can't you trust me and tell me what you're thinking and feeling? I wish you could know I can be trusted. I won't hurt you like other men have. At times, I get angry at you for shutting me out. I get angry and deeply hurt when you avoid having sex with me. It's not sex for me. It's making love, and I need it on a regular basis. I think you need it, too.

It's been my mistake to not tell you my true feelings and thoughts about your depression. I've stuffed, too. From now on, I'll be honest with you.

The truth is, our marriage is not very good. I'm not happy and satisfied in it. I'm battling to hang in there and continue to express love for you. But it's not easy.

I'm not going anywhere, and I never want a divorce. But I can't stand that we're not in a close, intimate marriage. It feels like I'm living with a roommate—an irritable, depressed, sad, tired roommate.

You need to know you're losing the kids. Your depression is driving them away more and more. They're losing respect for you. They're losing love for you. They can't depend on a mother who is cranky, critical, blows up unpredictably, and is too tired to spend time with them. Pretty soon they'll stop asking you to be with them. They're learning now to live their lives without you.

Sweetheart, I still love you and want a great marriage with you. I'm just weary. Work this process of recovery and get better. Please include me in the healing steps. I want to be a big part of helping you get rid of this depression.

In our next session, my client told me the letters had been read in two meetings: one with her spouse and pastor, and one with her and her accountability partner. As she described the meetings and the impact on her, it was obvious she had turned the corner of motivation.

She was determined to destroy her depression and start living a different, healthy life. These were her words, "I'm sick to death of my depression. I hate it. It's cost me everything. It's still costing me. I'll do whatever it takes to get well."

My response: "Good. You're ready for the next step."

Do Your Work

1. Pray that God will reveal your problem's payoffs. List them on paper. Read your list to your accountability partner and spouse and ask for their feedback.

2. Write a letter describing the high price of your problem in the past, present, and future.

3. Be specific and detailed. Ask your support team members to pray that you'll do a good job.

4. Ask key support team members to write letters describing what your problem is costing you and them. Ask your accountability partner. If you're married, ask your spouse. If you have a good relationship with your pastor and he knows you well, ask him.

5. Meet with your team members, together or one at a time, and listen to their letters. Read yours.

6. Ask yourself again: How much do you hate your problem? Are you in godly sorrow over your unhealthy behavior? How badly do you want to get better? Are you willing to do whatever it takes to get well?

CHAPTER 7

I WANT TO BE FREE:
HOW TO BEAT AN ADDICTION

"Doc, I've had two DUIs in the past six months. My driver's license is suspended, I'm barely hanging on to my job, and my wife is on the verge of leaving me. I've got to stop drinking before my whole life goes down the drain."

"I did a lot of pot in high school, college, and into my twenties. It seemed harmless enough, but cocaine is something else. It's ruining me. I crave it and continue to use even though I know it will cost me everything."

"I can't tell you how powerful the rush is when I go into the casino. I feel alive, passionate, and filled with energy. I also can't tell you how drained, stupid, and guilty I feel when I leave the casino. I'm twenty thousand dollars in the red, and I can't tell my wife."

"When I'm unhappy, I shop. When I'm stressed, I shop. When I have an argument with my husband, I shop. When I'm bored, I shop. I have more clothes than I could ever wear, and I've maxed out two credit cards. My husband's patience has run out."

"I've battled with my weight ever since junior high. I've tried every diet program you've ever heard of, all without success. My willpower is zero. I feel fat, ugly, and like a total failure."

"I always thought being a hard worker was a good thing. It's what my dad did. I've had time to think about my work ethic since my wife left me two weeks ago. She said I was married to my job, not her."

"My wife found out about the porn sites I've been visiting

on the Internet. She's furious, terribly hurt, and has kicked me out of the bedroom. I've got to stop my pornography habit, or I'll lose her for sure."

Addiction Is Everywhere

These are the stories of addicts. They are slaves to behaviors that are destroying their lives. They want to be free, but they cannot break the powerful hold their habit has on them. They pray. They make promises to God and loved ones that they'll stop. They grit their teeth and rely on determination and willpower. But sooner or later (usually sooner) they go back to their habit.

The number of addicts is skyrocketing. Millions of lives, marriages, and families—inside and outside the church—are being ruined by addiction. Something needs to be done.

That something is recovery. Addictions can be defeated with God's help, tremendous effort, and the correct steps of healing. It's time to take back your life and your relationships from your addiction. Enough is enough. You've wasted too many years chasing the false passion and bogus intimacy promised by your addiction.

My recovery program works for addictions, but there are a few extra actions addicts must take. I'll illustrate these extra steps by telling the story of a male sexual addict. I have chosen sexual addiction because it is the most common addiction for men.

The Ugly Cost of Pornography

As his wife cried silent tears on my couch, the man told me his story. He was a Christian. Married over twenty years. Three kids. Regular church attender. Addicted to pornography.

Just last week, his wife accidentally discovered the dozens of pornographic Web sites he had visited on their home computer. When he came home that evening and saw the look on her face, he knew something was terribly wrong. They stayed up all night talking and crying. He told me his whole life had been turned upside down, and it was his own stupid fault.

"Doc, pornography has been a part of my life since high school. It started with magazines, went to videos, spread to cable television, and now I'm hooked on Internet porn. Pornography has damaged every area of my life: my marriage, my kids, my job, and my relationship with God. I've got to stop. Can you help me?"

I told him, "Yes, you can beat this addiction if you're willing to work as hard as you've ever worked in your life. God will heal you through a series of specific and difficult recovery steps. If you refuse to do any of these steps, I'll stop therapy with you immediately. Are you willing to do everything I tell you?"

He said yes, so we got to work.

Support Team
The first thing we established was his support team. I required him to have *two* male accountability partners. Addicts are fighting patterns that are amazingly strong, so their accountability must be beefed up. He ended up choosing a close friend from church and a guy from his twelve-step sexual addiction group. He told them everything he'd done in his life in the sexual addiction area.

If at all possible, one of the accountability partners should have the same addiction as you. With a fellow addict on the job, you won't be able to fake it. You won't get away with anything because your partner knows all the addict tricks. He'll ask the right questions. He'll notice things a nonaddict will miss. He'll understand what you're going through. He'll nail you. That's what you need.

I told my client to meet in person at least once a week with each of his accountability partners. Addiction is too strong and sneaky to be held accountable over the phone. In-person meetings are essential for at least one year.

For an addict, a twelve-step group isn't optional. It's absolutely critical. Addicts rarely recover without going to a weekly addiction group for a minimum of one year. The power of a Christ-centered twelve-step group cannot be overstated. I told this man to find one and quick, which he did.

I also told him to meet with his pastor and tell him everything about his sexual addiction and to ask his pastor to create a spiritual growth program for him that would last at least one year. Even though his faith was weak at the time, he had to start rebuilding it. It could be a small men's Bible study or a one-on-one discipleship relationship with the pastor or a godly older man in the church. This pastor put him in an early morning men's Bible study. I had him tell these men his story of sexual addiction. Three more Christian men praying for him and holding him accountable couldn't hurt.

In his first therapy session, I signed up his wife as a support-team member. It was important that they heal together. I made two things about her role clear. First, she had to heal from the terrible wounds of his sexual sin before she could become a fully supportive and encouraging partner. When she was sufficiently healed and he had proved he was well on his way to recovery, then she could truly join him in the healing process. Until that time—I estimated it would take three to four months—he'd have to find empathy and warmth and positive words from his other support team members.

Second, she would not ever hear the struggles going on in his mind. His day-to-day fantasies and temptations would be shared with his two accountability partners, his twelve-step group, and his men's Bible study group. These thoughts would overwhelm her with pain and continue to rip open the wounds in her heart. However, if he acted out in any sexual way, then he'd have to tell her what he did.

The Document of Sin

With his support team assembled, I gave him his first assignment—a real doozy. I asked him to write a document of sexual sin, a letter to his wife in which he described all his sinful sexual behavior during their marriage from their wedding day to that day in as much detail as possible. He'd read this letter out loud to his wife in our next session.

An addict must confess his sin, in writing, to the person he is closest to in the world. In twenty years of clinical practice, I have seen this approach work thousands of times. In fact, I have never seen an addict recover without doing this assignment.

When the addict sees and feels the horrific impact of his sin on his precious loved one, he finally gets it. All his excuses and rationalizations evaporate. He is broken and repentant. He is motivated to change. If the addict is married, this written confession will be to the spouse. If not married, it should be read to that family member or friend to whom he is closest and loves the most.

This process is important for the spouse's healing. The addict isn't the only one who has to recover. The spouse can't forgive until she knows exactly what happened. She can't forgive what she doesn't know. And until he tells her all of his sins, she will always wonder what actually took place. This is Trauma Work 101: You don't heal until you know the details of the trauma.

This document of sins begins the restoration of the marriage. As the marriage is healing, the spouse can come alongside the addict, and they can become one flesh in the recovery. Plus, the intimacy they create during the recovery will meet one of the central needs of the addict. All addictions are a search for intimacy. By going through the steps of recovery with his spouse, the addict will find what he so desperately needs: intimacy with God and his marriage partner.

Here is an abbreviated version of this sexual addict's document of sexual sin:

I am so terribly sorry for all my sexual sins. I never realized how much I was hurting you with my disgusting behavior. I know now what I've done to you, and it's killing me inside. I've told you verbally what I've done, and now I'm putting it in writing.

Honey, let me say first that these behaviors are all my fault. One hundred percent my fault. You had nothing to do with my actions. I had this sexual addiction problem before I even met you, and I brought it with me into our marriage. I should have told you the truth and gotten help years ago. I chose to lie to myself and to you, and now we're both paying a huge price for my foolishness.

During the first two years of our marriage, I didn't use any pornography. I was so happy with you and my problem went underground. But after our first child was born, I went back to my old ways. The stress of fatherhood, my new career, and missing your time and attention may have been triggers. But there's no excuse. I decided to go back to pornography.

Our baby was about three months old when I started staying up late watching nasty, nudity-filled cable television shows. You'd be surprised what you can find on TV late at night. Movies, public access shows, and the Playboy channel were my favorites. Some channels, like the Playboy one, we didn't subscribe to, but they still came in clear enough to see. I'd usually stay up late on Friday or Saturday nights because

I could sleep in the next day. I'd watch for two or three hours, masturbate, then come to bed. I'm sorry. I was stupid.

I would occasionally get a pornographic magazine or two at a certain small grocery store. No one knew me there. This happened about once a month. I'd hide these magazines in my briefcase and look at them when you were out of the house or sleeping. After masturbating, I'd throw them in a dumpster on my way to work. Dumb. So dumb.

For about six years on and off, I'd buy pornographic videos from a seedy video store. About once every two months, I'd go in and buy two. They only cost about ten dollars each. Here are the titles of the ones I remember: [he listed them]. I'd watch these in the middle of the night, masturbate, and then come to bed. I would then throw them in the dumpster on my way to work the next day.

After each episode of viewing pornography and masturbating, I'd feel horribly guilty. I'd beg for God's forgiveness and promise to stop. I could last about two weeks before I started again. I know this sounds pathetic. The addiction had me totally under its control. It was my own stupid fault that I didn't admit my helplessness and get help. The truth is, I wanted to continue.

As you now know, five years ago I started viewing pornography on the Internet. This was like opening the floodgates to my sexual sin. It was bad and harmful before the Internet. After, it became much worse. I couldn't believe how easy it was to find pornography on the Web. The number of sites seemed endless, the variety was incredible, and most of it was free.

Magazines, television, and porno movies fell to the wayside as I got into Internet porn sites. Late at night or when you and the kids were out of the house, I'd visit these sites. I felt safe because you weren't too computer savvy. Most weeks, I'd view Internet porn about every three or four days. More on the weekends because I had more time.

I'd spend hours, sometimes three or four in a row, surfing porn sites. Friday night, Saturday night, and usually Sunday afternoon—these were my usual times. But then I started viewing Internet porn on weeknights. I couldn't seem to control myself. Here are the sites I can recall visiting: [he listed them]. I know you printed out a list of most of the ones I visited in the last three months.

I have to tell you something you don't know yet. I went to two strip clubs this last year. [He named them.] Both times, I watched the girls dance for about thirty minutes and then left. I guess I wanted the rush of seeing naked women in person. Anyway, it didn't do much for me. They weren't attractive, and I spent the whole time scared to death someone I knew would see me.

Well, that's it. I'm ashamed beyond words of what I've done. I'm sorry, so very sorry for my sin. I know I have hurt you worse than anyone has ever hurt you. I know you will have to vent your feelings and ask me questions for a while. I will listen and answer all your questions for as long as it takes. I will do whatever it takes to fix this problem and win you back. Please, please, please hang in there with me as I work through to recovery.

When he read this letter to his wife in session, it was very intense and very painful. It needed to be. Both were in tears before he finished. The process blew up Satan's lie that his sexual behavior wasn't hurting anyone. The healing for both of them had begun.

I instructed him to read this letter as soon as possible to his two accountability partners, his twelve-step group, his pastor, and the three men in his Bible study group. I asked his wife to read the letter to her closest female friend. She needed empathy and prayer support from a trusted confidante who knew the hurts she had suffered.

The Document of Response
I told his wife it was now her turn to write a letter to her husband. A letter containing her response to what he had done to her. A letter expressing, without limitation or qualification, her emotional pain, rage, hurt, disgust, anger, resentment, frustration, sadness. I urged her to not hold back because full and honest release of emotion is a critical part of the forgiveness process.

She wrote ten pages straight from her heart. Here are key portions of her response:

> I don't know if I can find the words to describe what you've done to me with your sexual sin. You have hurt me like no one else could. You have broken my heart, and I don't know if it can be healed.
>
> I feel like I don't even know you. In fact, I don't want to know the person who did all these miserable, hurtful actions. Here's what I do know: You have lost me. There's a good chance you won't get me back. If you want to win me back, you'd better work like no man has ever worked to change and become the godly husband I want and need.
>
> You see, I thought I had a godly husband. Turns out, I didn't. I had a husband who defiled himself, me, our kids, and our marriage over and over again.
>
> My initial shock has turned to rage. How could you keep doing things you knew were wrong? How could you lie and

deceive me for all these years? I am beyond furious at you.
You have been so selfish it makes me sick. Why didn't you get
help? Why didn't you tell someone?

I think of you watching naked women, and I want to
scream in your face, "What are you doing? You've got a wife
who loves you! You can see me naked and make love to me!"
But no, you took what was mine alone and gave it to these
anonymous whores.

I am shaking with anger as I write these words. And
underneath the anger is a terrible hurt and sadness. You
have wounded me just as if you'd taken a knife and gutted
me with it. You, who were supposed to protect and honor me.
Instead, you've damaged me and humiliated me.

I've cried and cried and cried. I feel like I have been torn
apart and don't know how I can be put back together again.
I don't trust you. I don't feel safe with you. I don't know if I
love you. I've taken my heart, my broken and bleeding heart,
away from you.

Do your work. Follow the steps of recovery to the letter.
Let me know how the process is going. Listen to me every
time I want to talk about what you've done. Hear me vent
and feel my pain. Answer all my questions. Grow in the
Lord. You can't change without His help.

I don't offer you any guarantees. "We'll see" is the best I
can do.

It was pure agony for both of them when she read this letter in
our session. But it was the truth. And the truth heals. She had to
say it, and he had to hear it. You'll notice there was no empathy
or understanding in her response letter. It was venting about his
sin and the pain he had caused her. Nothing else. Emotional
expression must come first.

She was a step closer to forgiveness and to becoming a partner in his healing process.

The Mode

The next step for the addict and his spouse was what I call *the mode*, a series of brutally honest, intense, and deeply personal conversations about his sexual behavior. The spouse could ask to have one of these talks at any time and the addict's response—every time—would always have to be, "Yes, let's talk."

I told the spouse that her job was to use these talks to vent her emotions as freely and completely as possible. She was also to ask all the questions that came into her head, with the exception of his fantasies and temptations.

His job in the face of these confrontations was to be patient, kind, loving, understanding, and reassuring. He was to say he was sorry a million and one times—and mean it every time. He was to do his best to answer all her questions, even when she repeated them over and over. Specific questions about why and how he developed the addiction would be answered as they worked through the rest of the recovery steps.

The one-two-three punch of the two documents and the mode accelerates the healing of the addict, the spouse, and the relationship. For a more complete explanation of this approach to serious marital sin, read my book, *What To Do When Your Spouse Says, I Don't Love You Anymore* (Nelson, 2002).

Cut Off Avenues to Addiction

The addict must work with his support team to take aggressive actions to limit his access to the addiction. For the sexual addict, this means never watching television alone at home, never turning on the television when in a hotel room, having a filter on his computer, only using the computer when his spouse is home and she uses the secret password to get online, never visiting a video store alone, avoiding the magazine racks at convenience stores and grocery stores and bookstores, and going to bed every night at the same time as his wife.

The Rest of the Story

His autobiography revealed the sources of his sexual addiction and how it had grown over the years leading up to his marriage. Both his parents had unwittingly made huge contributions to the birth of his addiction. He never connected with his mom. She was a cold, unaffectionate person who was critical. He never forgot the day she made fun of the size of his penis. His dad was gone a lot, did not model how to be a man, and had a porn stash in the garage.

His female second grade teacher didn't like him and regularly made him the focus of her jokes. She criticized his academic work and provided almost zero encouragement. One day, she embarrassed him in front of the entire class. Adding to his rejection by females were two girlfriends who rejected him in junior high.

When he came across his dad's pornographic magazines and movies, he found a way to cope with his pain and stress. Looking at naked women gave him a rush he had never experienced. He felt confident and in control. He was quickly hooked.

He completed the steps connected to the autobiography and calculated the high cost of his addiction. He, like my depressed client, was ready to move on.

I told them both, "Now we need to fix your brain."

Do Your Work

1. Commit to building your support team: two same-sex accountability partners, a twelve-step group, your pastor, a spiritual-growth discipleship relationship or small group Bible study, and your spouse.

2. Write your document of sin to your spouse or, if not married, to the person you love the most in the world. Read it out loud to this special person and then to the other members of your support team.

3. Ask your special, loved person to write and then read to you the document of response.

4. Begin the mode with your loved one and agree to continue it as long as it takes to produce healing.

5. Take the necessary steps to cut off avenues to your addiction.

CHAPTER 8

THERE'S SOMETHING WRONG WITH YOUR MIND: IF YOU THINK CRAZY, YOU'LL ACT CRAZY

Here are some crazy stories from the news about the way people think:

- A man stole a car from a gas station. The owner had left his car at the gas pump to go inside and prepay for the gas. He left the car unlocked with the keys in the ignition. The thief simply jumped in and took off. When he realized the tank was empty, the thief returned to the same gas station to fill up. He was met there by the police. Not exactly a criminal mastermind.

- A woman went to the same fast food restaurant twice a day for three years. She had a large hamburger, fries, and a shake at lunch and at dinner every day. She knew the manager and the workers by name. As a result of this diet, she developed serious health problems, including obesity, diabetes, and coronary heart disease. She sued the restaurant, claiming the staff should have warned her that their fatty food was endangering her health. Surprisingly, her lawsuit did not mention anyone holding a gun to her head and forcing her to gobble down these menu items.

- And now my all-time favorite: A young man strapped a refrigerator to his back and walked the course of a local footrace. He wanted to impress his friends with his strength and maybe get his picture in the paper. What he got was humiliation and severe injuries to his back. He sued the manufacturer of the refrigerator for failing to warn him of the potential consequences of carrying its product on his back. Obviously, there should have been a large warning label: Although it is tempting, do not carry this appliance on your back.

These are true stories! Isn't it hard to believe there are individuals who can distort the truth in such an outrageous fashion? Actually it shouldn't be hard to believe. We all distort the truth. And the results are equally disastrous for us.

Here are some stories of crazy thinking from my therapy office:

- A man and his wife, both in their early fifties, were worried about their thirty-year-old son. He still lived at home, had no job, wasn't looking for a job, and was terrorizing them in their own home. He stayed up late and slept in late every day, refused to do any chores, drank alcohol and used drugs in their home, and often cursed at them in fits of rage. They told me they felt sorry for their son and were trying to love him the way Jesus would. I said I felt sorry for *them* and that Jesus would have kicked their son out long ago.

- My client was a successful attorney who made well over half a million dollars a year. He was a partner in his firm, a brilliant courtroom strategist, and had earned a great reputation in the southeast region of the United States as a litigator in his area of expertise. He also had low self-esteem and was constantly tortured by insecurities and doubts. With a straight face, he told me he was an incompetent attorney and lived every day in fear that he would be exposed as a charlatan. I told him there were two possibilities: He was the greatest fake the legal profession had ever known, or his thinking was messed up.

- I sat with a married couple and listened patiently as the wife blamed herself for her husband's four-month affair. She said her weight, her over-involvement at church, her focus on the children, and her lack of interest in sex had driven this poor man to another woman. I said, "No, he drove in his Volvo to see her. Unless you held a gun to his head and forced him to have sex with what's her name, the affair is 100 percent *his* fault."

These clients of mine were reasonable, regular folks. Just like you. They weren't candidates for a rubber room in a mental hospital. Their crazy thinking didn't make the news. The errors of their thinking weren't public, obvious, and exaggerated like the three people whose activities made the news. Their thinking was private, subtle, and hidden. But just as real and just as serious.

Your Brain Has a Problem

I hate to be the bearer of more bad news, but that's my job. I tell people the truth, whether they want to hear it or not. In addition to having an emotional problem, you have a serious problem with your brain. You think in distorted, twisted ways. Of course, you're not the only one. Everyone does.

Let me present three pieces of evidence to prove my case about your messed up thinking.

First, I distort the truth with my mind. That probably doesn't come as a complete shock. Just recently at a family meeting, Sandy told me I was working too many hours, and she and the kids felt neglected. I was sure she was wrong and proceeded to spend ten minutes explaining how I was balancing work and family life. Sandy had the nerve to ask the children to tell me what they thought. They both told me I was working too much. I finally had to admit, after a few more minutes of defensive maneuvering, that I had been distorting the truth.

Second, I've never met anyone who didn't distort the truth. It's a universal problem. When I help clients examine their thinking, they don't say, "Wow, what a relief! Everything's fine here. My thoughts are as pure as the driven snow." They discover thinking problems that are driving their emotional problems.

Third, and the best evidence of all, scripture tells us that the mind is evil and distorts the truth. Read Jeremiah 17:9 and tell me what it says about your thinking: " 'The heart [here, indicating the mind] is more deceitful than all else and is desperately sick; who can understand it?' "

That about sums it up. Our minds are deceitful and sick and filled with lies.

We have plenty of company in scripture when it comes to Jeremiah 17:9. Look at this short list of biblical personalities and some of the lies they believed:

- *Adam and Eve:* We will be like God. We will be wise. We can sin and get away with it.

- *Abraham and Sarah:* God cannot be trusted. We won't be able to have a child.

- *Moses:* I'm not worthy. I'm not smart. I'm not articulate. I can't lead God's people.

- *David:* I can have sex with Bathsheba, and there will be no consequences.

- *Jonah:* I can run away from God, disobey Him, live life my way, and everything will be fine.

- *Paul (before he came to Christ):* I'm pleasing God by persecuting these Christians.

- *Peter:* Jesus can't protect me.

Sin nature affects every part of us, including our minds. If you want to get a gruesomely detailed description of the human mind's depraved condition and the sinful behavior that results, read Romans 1:18 through 3:20. It's all there, in living color.

Because the sin nature remains after trusting Christ, we continue to have thinking problems. An integral part of the sanctification process—growing closer to Jesus Christ—is changing our minds. A changed mind will lead to emotional, spiritual, and relational health.

Three Facts about Thinking

Thinking determines how you live

How you think is who you are: "For as he thinks within himself, so he is" (Proverbs 23:7). Your thinking determines your emotional responses, your behavior, your lifestyle, and the quality of your relationships.

Thinking is the key to change

You must renew your mind to be healthy, to make changes

in how you live, to grow emotionally and spiritually, and to become more like Jesus Christ. In Romans 12:1–2, God makes it clear what has to happen to your mind: "Therefore I urge you, brethren, by the mercies of God, to present your bodies a living and holy sacrifice, acceptable to God, which is your spiritual service of worship. And do not be conformed to this world, but be transformed by the renewing of your mind, so that you may prove what the will of God is, that which is good and acceptable and perfect."

How do you give your whole life to God as a sacrifice? How do you truly worship God? How do you avoid being conformed to this secular, Satan-centered world? How are you to transform? How do you live in the will of God? By renewing your mind.

How do you renew your mind? How do you change your thinking? The answer is found in the third fact about thinking.

Each person distorts the truth in specific, distinctive ways

The secret to renewing your mind is finding out how *you* distort the truth. The lies you believe—I call them *core lies*—are the major source of your emotional problem. Identifying and correcting these lies will be a huge step toward emotional and spiritual wholeness.

Every thought you have is not distorted. The deeply embedded core lies are the ones that need to be rooted out and replaced. Satan uses your lies to cripple and destroy you. God wants you to stop believing these lies and to start believing the truth. Knowing the truth will set you free (John 8:32).

Core Lies

What are core lies? They are entrenched incorrect thoughts

developed in childhood that determine the lifestyle used to cope with pain and meet personal needs.

Entrenched Incorrect Thoughts

Entrenched incorrect thoughts are set in concrete well before you begin a relationship with Jesus Christ. These thoughts are not true. They are lies. They're largely unconscious and operate outside of your awareness. They exist in clusters or groups. They are attached to the old nature within you.

Developed in Childhood

Your lies were created as a result of the pain from unmet needs (to be loved and valued, for instance) and from the teaching of your parents. If your father communicated the message that you were worthless, for example, you believed that lie because you had no choice—you were just a kid. The emotional trauma that comes with the lie gives it tremendous power and permanence, even into your adult life. The emotional pain is what makes the lie into a core lie.

Lifestyle Used to Cope

You build a way of life based on your core lies. Your lifestyle is how you express your emotions, how you behave, and how you operate in relationships. This is another name for your emotional problem. Your lifestyle, because it is fueled by lies, is an unsuccessful attempt to deal with painful events and get certain needs met.

Core Lie Patterns

I'll show you how all this works by describing four common patterns. See if any of these patterns sound familiar:

I'm Worthless

- Unmet needs created by parental teaching
  The parents are harsh, rejecting, critical.
  The parents are emotionally unavailable.
  Their message is *you are worthless and unlovable.*

- Core lies
  I am worthless and I always will be.
  I will never amount to anything.
  I will never be loved by anyone.
  I must not express my anger.

- Lifestyle
  I am depressed.
  I focus on the negative to confirm my worthlessness.
  I use failure to get attention.
  I have poor self-esteem.

I'm Just Not Good Enough

- Unmet needs created by parental teaching
  The parents are demanding and perfectionists.
  The parents rigidly control and offer little freedom.
  Their message is *you will never be good enough.*

- Core lies
  I must be perfect in every area of life.
  If I can be perfect, I'll be loved.
  I must be punctual, conscientious, orderly, and
    reliable in everything all the time.
  I must be in control, especially of my emotions.

- Lifestyle
    I am perfectionist, obsessive-compulsive, anxious.
    I am stressed, anxious, tense, worried.
    I am unable to relax.
    I am a workaholic.
    I have a stress-related physical disorder [lupus,
        chronic fatigue, migraines, etc.].

It's My Fault

- Unmet needs created by parental teaching
    The home is chaotic and confusing.
    The parents are unpredictable and in chronic
        conflict.
    The parents battle addictions.
    The parents are mentally unstable.
    Their message is *you are to blame for our problems*.

- Core lies
    I must save everyone from their pain.
    I am to blame for problems in my relationships.
    I can change another person if I try hard enough.
    I must not express my emotions and thoughts
        because that might alienate those I'm saving.

- Lifestyle
    I am a codependent rescuer.
    I focus on other's needs in an effort to rescue them.
    I tolerate mistreatment.
    I have an inability to create intimacy in a
        relationship.
    I married "a project."

- Unmet needs created by parental teaching
  Parents are dominant and controlling.
  Parents make the decisions for their children.
  Parents offer little love and do not express their
    emotions.
  Their message is *you are not able to think for yourself.*

- Core lies
  I must be loved and respected by everyone.
  I cannot tolerate rejection or conflict.
  I cannot make my own decisions.
  I must not honestly express my emotions and
    thoughts because others might not approve.

- Lifestyle
  I am a dependent people-pleaser.
  I always agree with thoughts or opinions expressed
    by others.
  I am passive or subassertive.
  I fear rejection.
  I have an addiction of my own.

You see how it works? Childhood pain (unmet needs created by parental teaching) leads to core lies that impact lifestyle. You may have noticed that one of the core lies in each pattern had to do with not expressing emotions. Expressing emotions in a healthy way is necessary to completely strip your core lies of their power. We'll consider this in more detail in a later chapter.

These are just four patterns of distorted thinking. There are hundreds, even thousands more. In fact, each of you has your own unique, distinctive cluster of core lies.

Rewiring Your Brain

Your negative, incorrect, and irrational core lies are deeply embedded in your brain. They've been in place and humming along at full capacity practically your whole life. It's going to take time and effort and the right strategy to dislodge them.

Some so-called experts say it takes thirty days to break a habit. Baloney! Who are they kidding? They're living in a fairyland. It will take three to six months to rewire your brain, but you'll be able to get it done—with God's help.

You need to identify your core lies and replace them with core truths. Core truths are entrenched correct thoughts based on an accurate view of self that determine the lifestyle used to serve and glorify God.

Ephesians 4:17–24 has a beautiful and powerful description of this process. First, we are taught to leave behind the old self with its lies, deceit, darkened understanding, and destructive behavior. Second, we are taught to put on the new self with its renewed mind, righteousness, truth, and healthy behavior.

Yes! That's exactly what I'm talking about! That's what we're going to learn to do in the next few chapters. We're going to leave behind your old self by getting rid of its core lies. We're going to build up your new self by installing God's core truths.

Do Your Work

1. Recall a time in your life when your crazy thinking led to crazy behavior. Tell this story to at least one member of your support team.

2. Does one of the four core lies patterns fit you? What do you think your core lies are? Ask a support team member for some input on what yours may be. Jot down some possible core lies, along with your lifestyle (your emotional problem), and your childhood pain.

3. Read Ephesians 4:17–24 three times and meditate on it for a few minutes. Pray that God will help you identify your core lies.

CHAPTER 9

HAVE YOUR HEAD EXAMINED:
THE LIES YOU LIVE BY

My depressed client had completed her autobiography and answered the twelve questions connected to it. She had figured out her depression's payoffs. Through her own letter and the letters written by her team members, she had fully realized the high price of her depression.

Now it was time to show her how her negative, irrational thoughts—her lies—were controlling and ruining her life. I told her the lies she was taught as a child were still operating at full strength. And they would continue to operate until she learned how to identify them, refute them, and replace them with God's truth.

The Core Lies in the Autobiography

I had her dust off her autobiography, and we took a close look at it. It was easy for her to figure out that her core lie pattern was *I am worthless*. She believed that big, fat lie completely. It was lodged in her brain and had been there for decades. It wouldn't be easy to shake it loose.

I asked her to go home, carefully study her autobiography, and identify the core lies in it. I urged her to ask these individuals to help in this project: God (through prayer for His wisdom and insight), her husband, and her accountability partner.

It took her two weeks, but she came up with a good, solid list of core lies. Most of the lies came straight out of her autobiography. Some were revealed to her by God. Some came from her husband and accountability partner. Her core lies fell into five categories:

View of Self

- I'll never be good enough.

- I'm not pretty.

- I'm stupid.

- I'm not good at anything.

- My abortion proves I'm a bad person.

- I'll always be depressed.

View of Others

- I'll never be loved.

- I'll never be able to trust a man.

- Sex is dirty and shameful.

- I can't make good, close friends.

- Others think negatively about me.

- If others know the truth about me, they'll reject me.

- I can't ever be close to my husband, my kids, or anyone.

View of Emotions and Opinions

- I must stuff all difficult emotions, especially anger, with adults.

- I must never share my opinions.

- My opinions are wrong.

- I must avoid conflict with adults and keep the peace at all times.

- I'm angry and hurt at my dad, my abuser, and my ex-boyfriend, but I can't ever express these emotions.

View of Life

- I can't take risks.

- I won't ever be a success, so there's no point even trying new things.

- I must settle for mediocrity.

- I must play it safe in life.

View of God

- God is punishing me for having premarital sex.

- God is punishing me for having an abortion.

- God doesn't love me.

- At best, God tolerates me.

- God doesn't want to be close to me.

- God can't and won't use me in His service.

She was amazed at the number of core lies that were on her list. It wasn't a complete list, but it was a good working inventory of her lies. Her big lie, *I am worthless*, had branched out into many other lies over the years. As we studied her list, she realized that she still believed every one of the lies. Each lie did its part to keep her depression strong and robust.

Thinking as a Child

I told her, "You're still thinking as a child." She was insulted and wanted to know what I was talking about. I explained that most of her core lies were learned as she grew up. Once each lie was learned, it became a permanent part of her thinking. Since she still believed all her lies, she still was thinking as a child.

For example, at five years old her dad taught her she would never be good enough. Every time she believes that lie as an adult, she is thinking like a five-year-old. A five-year-old thinks, "If my dad says I'll never be good enough, it must be true."

A grown woman in her thirties or forties (or fifties or sixties or seventies) would be able to deny that lie if her dad told it to her today. But it's too late. The lie learned by the five-year-old is set in concrete and will follow the person forever—or until that lie is identified and defeated.

The Father of Lies on the Job

Spiritual warfare is real. Very real. In Ephesians 6:11–12, the Bible makes it clear that Satan and his evil forces are our main enemies in life: "Put on the full armor of God, so that you will be able to stand firm against the schemes of the devil. For our struggle is not against flesh and blood, but against the rulers, against the powers, against the world forces of this darkness, against the spiritual forces of wickedness in the heavenly places."

If the word picture in 1 Peter 5:8 doesn't get your full attention, nothing will: "Be of sober spirit, be on the alert. Your adversary, the devil, prowls about like a roaring lion, seeking someone to devour."

Guess who Satan wants to devour? That's right. You. Your picture and bio are on his bulletin board in hell and Satan will cook up all kinds of schemes (2 Corinthians 2:11) and throw flaming arrows (Ephesians 6:16) to destroy you. Satan's not kidding around. He intends to rip you—and all you hold dear—to pieces.

My depressed client asked me, "How do you think Satan will try to devour me?"

I told her, "He's already doing a bang-up job of devouring you with your depression. And his main assault weapon is the lies you believe. He's been very successful because you think your lies are the truth."

Satan has been lying ever since the creation of man and woman (Genesis 3:1–13). He deceives the whole world (Revelation 12:9). Jesus calls him "a liar and the father of lies" (John 8:44).

I told my client that Satan knew the lies in her mind, and he was working overtime, every day, to encourage and support those lies. As Adam and Eve found out, he is also fully capable of making up his own lies and whispering them to us.

Her struggle against her lies was an emotional battle *and* a spiritual battle. To fight back and begin to make some progress in her emotional and spiritual health, I told her she needed to first learn how to identify her lies.

Verbal Confrontation of the Lies

The first method of identification is verbal confrontation. I asked her to tell me about painful current events in her life. My job was to point out the lies she told in each story and their negative impact. I also had her sign up her husband and accountability partner to do the same job. Eventually she'd learn how to identify her own lies in every situation and clearly see how they were ruining her life.

Here are some examples from my interactions with her:

I'm Not Pretty

Client: I went to a parent-teacher meeting at school two days ago. Man, what a bummer! I walked in, and I swear, every woman there looked like a million dollars: thin, glamorous, great makeup, stylish clothes, hair just right. And there I was, Mrs. Frumpy. My hair was a mess, twenty extra pounds on my stomach and thighs, wrinkled blouse and skirt, and looking old and tired. I wish I could be half as attractive as those ladies.

Me: You just told two lies. One, I doubt if every single woman there was a gorgeous babe. What was it, a meeting of Miss America contestants? The second lie is the big one, though. *I'm not pretty.* And not just *not pretty.* You believe the lie that you're downright ugly. Tell me, what did this second lie do to your self-image and frame of mind?

Client: Well, I felt ugly and totally inferior that evening and all the next day. Depressed, too.

Me: Ugly and depressed. That's what the I'm-not-pretty lie will do for you.

I'm Stupid

Client: You won't believe what happened at work the other day. My boss had asked me to do three specific things, and I did two but forgot the third. We're in a staff meeting, and he asked me about the third thing. I wanted to crawl under the desk. I was mortified and humiliated. I am so stupid. How could I have forgotten? He didn't seem too upset about it, but I just know he was angry and disappointed. He must think I'm an airhead who can't be trusted. I wonder how long it'll be before he realizes how incompetent I am and fires me.

Me: Whoa, you'd better stop right there. I'm having a hard time keeping track of all your lies. The main lie is *I'm stupid.* Here are other lies:

1. Your boss was angry and disappointed.

2. Your boss thinks you're an untrustworthy airhead.

3. You're incompetent.

4. He will fire you any time now.

What was the impact of these lies?

Client: I was really depressed for two days. Worse than usual. Plus I was worried about looking bad in front of the office staff and maybe even losing my job.

Me: Interesting, isn't it? You are so good at depressing yourself and getting in a panic over your job. And all this over a pack of lies. You made the whole crisis up in your head, with some help from Satan.

I Can't Make Good, Close Friends
Client: I went to a women's social at church, and it didn't go well. I got there late, and I kind of hung out by the snack table. A few ladies did come and speak to me, but I don't think they found me too interesting. I didn't participate in the games they played, and I said next to nothing in the small group. I didn't bother signing up for

any of the Bible studies. People don't seem to like me. I try and try, but I just can't make any good, close friends.

Me: I hear four lies in this scenario, too.

1. You're uninteresting.

2. You're unlikable.

3. You try and try.

4. You conclude, based on your previous three lies, that you can't make any good, close friends.

I wonder how your bad experience at this party made you feel?

Client: Worthless, friendless, depressed, and not willing to go to any other socials for a while.

Me: Good work. You planned for total failure, and you succeeded in achieving it. Your lies make sure you stay virtually friendless. That feeds your depression, and you can continue to believe you'll never make any friends.

I Must Stuff All Difficult Emotions, Especially Anger
Client: My husband refused to help me with an important home project and, even worse, made some critical and insensitive remarks to me. I was very hurt. I didn't say anything to him because it wouldn't have done any good. I can't do conflict. If I spoke up, it would only make the situation worse. I guess I'm a peacemaker. Plus he's a good guy and probably didn't mean what he said.

Me: Hurt? That's only partially true. You were angry, but you can't admit that or express it yet. You did a masterful job of talking yourself out of being honest with your husband. Listen to your trail of lies:

1. I was *only* hurt.

2. Verbalizing my emotions wouldn't have helped.

3. I can't handle conflict.

4. Being honest would make it worse.

5. And the biggest lie of all, I'm a peacemaker.

What did these lies do to you and your relationship with your husband?

Client: I felt terrible the rest of that day. Down. Blue. Sad. I yelled at the kids for messing up the house. I avoided my husband, and when he asked for sex that night, I told him I had a headache. That was another lie, wasn't it?

Me: Can you see what stuffing your anger does to you and those you love? You stay depressed and take it out on your kids and your husband. You think terrible things will happen if you express your anger. The truth is, terrible things happen if you don't express it.

Many of these lies are easy to spot, aren't they? They seem obvious when they're written down on paper. But her lies were not obvious to my client. She believed they were true, and she lived her life by them. Her lies had been her constant companions for over thirty years. Getting her to speak the lies out loud to me, her husband, and her accountability partner was a critical first step in killing them. When her lies were just in her head and no one knew about them but her (and Satan), they had great power. When she spoke her lies out loud, they were exposed and weakened.

The Three Columns

After a few weeks of being orally confronted with her lies, she was ready to begin writing her lies. I told her that putting her lies on paper would further expose and weaken them. Writing would force her to take responsibility for the process of identifying her lies and seeing their destructive impact on her life. By writing her lies, she was taking the lead role in her own emotional healing.

I call this writing technique *the three columns*. Buy a spiral notebook and divide each page into three columns and label them with the *three whats*:

- *What happened?* Write a brief description of the event. Just hit the highlights.

- *What did you think and feel?* Write your thoughts about what happened. What did it mean to you? This is where your lies will show up. Jot down your emotional reaction to the event.

- *What was the result?* What did you do? What did you say? What impact did the event have on you?

You carry your notebook with you wherever you go. When an event occurs that is painful or difficult, take out your notebook as soon as you can and jot down information in the three columns. It's important to record these specific bits of data while they're still fresh in your mind. Then sit down with one of your support team members and read your description of the event. Try to share this information the same day it happens or at least within two days of the event. If you can't sit down together in person, share your information over the phone.

The writing and talking of the three-column approach will accelerate your ability to spot your lies and to clearly see the mess your lies are making of your life. By writing you're taking control of your healing. By sharing you're able to get feedback from individuals who care about you and will speak truth to you. If you did a good job identifying your lies and their impact, they'll tell you that. If you missed a lie or downplayed a lie's impact, they'll tell you that, too.

Here are two events my depressed client used the three columns to describe:

What happened?	What did you think and feel?	What was the result?
I forgot to show up at my son's school fund-raiser. I had volunteered, but it slipped my mind. My son was disappointed. I got an e-mail from the volunteer coordinator saying, "Where were you?"	I felt embarrassed and angry at myself. I'm stupid, irresponsible, and a bad mom (lies).	I was depressed for two days. I said I'm sorry to my son. I e-mailed some bogus reasons to the volunteer coordinator.

What happened?	What did you think and feel?	What was the result?
I heard a sermon Sunday on the evils of abortion. The pastor made it clear abortion is the murder of an innocent child.	I was devastated, felt horribly guilty, and cried all during the sermon. I killed someone and can't be forgiven (the second part is a lie). I'm a bad person (a lie). God is still punishing me for my abortion (a lie). I deserve to be depressed (a lie).	I had bad depression for a week. My husband tried to get me to talk, but I refused. I stuffed my feelings. I ate too much to try and escape the pain. I felt bad about gaining weight.

Do you get the idea? Because my client had been confronted with her lies during one of our sessions first, she was better able to spot her lies as she used the three-column writing technique. She read each of these events to me, her husband, and her accountability partner and those sessions helped her talk out her lies and emotions more fully. She was getting the hang of catching herself in her lies. She was realizing more and more the awful impact of her lies.

Now she was prepared to go to the next level in her war against Satan and her lies. It was time for her to learn how to aggressively challenge her lies and replace them with truths. God's truths.

And I was just the guy to help her.

Do Your Work

1. Carefully study your autobiography and jot down all the core lies in it. Ask God and a support team member for help and input.

2. Do you believe that Satan is your number one enemy? Can you see how he is using your lies to destroy you? Pray that God would give you the power and insight needed to defeat Satan.

3. For one week, try the strategy of confronting your lies with your spouse or your accountability partner or both. Talk through difficult or painful events with these support team members and ask them to help you identify your lies.

4. For one or two weeks, use the three-column technique to expose your lies and their destructive force in your life. Jot down the three columns of information for each event and share your thoughts with a support team member.

CHAPTER 10

TAKE EVERY THOUGHT CAPTIVE:
THINK ACCURATELY AND BIBLICALLY

I am not a handy person. I can't fix anything. The one home improvement task I can handle is changing lightbulbs. I'm not kidding. I have the mechanical aptitude of a rock. Well, not even as high as a rock; I don't want to insult rocks.

Sandy can do just about anything with her hands. When I try to do a home project, it almost always turns out disastrously. I throw my tools, have my usual yelling fit, and Sandy has to come in and complete the project. Do you know how humiliating that is?

Recently, my son, William, was playing in the yard with his buddies, Hunter and Daylin. He came inside and said, "Dad, the chain on Daylin's bike slipped off. Can you fix it?" Sandy was busy making cookies, so he didn't bother her. Cookies are one of the main food groups in the Clarke household.

After I recovered from my shock at even being asked to help with a bike chain, I immediately had a string of negative, inaccurate thoughts: *I can't fix that bike; it's a waste of time to even try; you'll be embarrassed in front of the boys; you'll snap the chain and have to pay for it.*

I sent William outside, and I said to Sandy: "What, is he crazy? I've never fixed a bike chain in my life. I've never fixed anything in my life."

She calmly looked at me and replied, "Well, it can't hurt to try, can it?"

That comment got my attention. I realized my thoughts were lies. Nasty, ridiculous, confidence-sapping lies. As I gathered a few tools, I fought back against my lies and corrected them with the truth:

- *Maybe I can fix that bike. Philippians 4:13 says I can do anything with the power of Jesus Christ.*

- *No, it's not a waste of time. William and Daylin will appreciate my effort no matter what happens. I'm showing kindness.*

- *I won't be embarrassed. My worth doesn't depend on fixing a bike. Plus, the guys won't care. Their attention spans are only two minutes anyway.*

- *It's unlikely I'll break the chain. If I do, so what? Buying a new one won't break the bank.*

My new, accurate, and true thoughts gave me confidence and motivation. I went outside, and with the boys watching, I diagnosed the problem. The chain was wedged tightly between the circle thingy and the fender thingy. I used a screwdriver from my trusty five-piece home tool set and dislodged it. I carefully threaded the chain back on the ridged thingies. I fixed that bike!

Respect! Success! Victory! A plate of cookies from my admiring wife! Instant status as a neighborhood dad who could fix bike chains! And all because I got rid of my self-defeating lies and inserted positive, accurate truths.

My bike experience is a small example of what you must do to reach the next level of correct, healthy thinking. The first level is identifying your lies and realizing their impact on your life. The second level, the focus of this chapter, is aggressively attacking your lies and replacing them with God's truth.

Second Corinthians 10:5 describes what God wants you to do with all your thoughts: "taking every thought captive to the obedience of Christ." In the context of this verse, Paul says that Christians are in a war. An all-out, vicious, high-stakes spiritual war. This war is not only against false prophets and their heretical beliefs, but also against all the lies Satan launches into our minds. The key to winning the war is refuting Satan's lies and believing God's truths.

Go to War Against Your Lies

I told my depressed client that it was time for her to go to war against her lies. Her lies were strong and deeply entrenched in her mind. They were set in concrete and needed to be broken with a jackhammer.

She asked, "How do I go to war?"

I explained that she had to mount an aggressive, no-holds-barred attack against her lies. Being nice or even kind of mean wouldn't even touch them. She needed to be fed up, disgusted, and angry at her lies. I was going to teach her to treat her lies with toughness, rudeness, meanness, biting humor, sarcasm, and ridicule.

"Is this approach biblical?" she asked.

"You'd better believe it is," I responded.

The Bible and Guerrilla Warfare

An important theme of the Bible is confronting sin in all its forms and replacing it with God's truth. This process is crucial for spiritual and emotional health. That's what I'm recommending. Your lies are sin, and you, with God's help, must work hard to confront them and to shred them, and then to hold firm to God's truths.

Jesus confronted lies with bluntness, passion, and anger. Matthew 4:1–11 tells the story of how Jesus used scripture to defeat Satan's lies and schemes when He was being tested in the wilderness. In Matthew 4:10 (ESV), Jesus says, "Be gone, Satan!" That sounds pretty angry and aggressive, doesn't it? Jesus didn't politely ask Satan to leave. He firmly and passionately told him to buzz off.

In Matthew 23:1–36, Jesus absolutely ripped the Pharisees and their lies to pieces. These verses contain some of the strongest, most brutal and sarcastic words in the Bible. He was publicly gouging the revered religious leaders of the day. Jesus didn't care. They were liars and hypocrites and He called them on these sins.

The apostle Paul fiercely and angrily went after lies. In Galatians 3:1, he uses strong language: "You foolish Galatians!" That wasn't nice, was it? Paul wanted to offend them, shake them up, and get their attention. The Galatians were believing lies about important spiritual matters, and Paul repeatedly battered those lies.

In Galatians 2:11–21, Paul confronted Peter face-to-face over Peter's sin of hypocrisy and not living out the truth of the gospel. Paul's confrontation was direct, blunt, and effective.

Prepare for Battle

I went after my depressed client's lies in a forceful and aggressive way. I wanted to beat her lies to a pulp and get God's truths into her brain. I had her sign up two other individuals on her lie-bashing team: her husband and her accountability partner. As she reported events and expressed lies to them, their job was to go after those lies in hand-to-hand combat.

The ultimate goal was to teach her to do this lie-removal and truth-replacement process on her own.

For this kind of warfare to be successful, three preparatory steps are important. First, you carefully choose the individuals you will ask to challenge your lies. These must be people you have a safe, trusting relationship with. The process gets a little ugly, and you need to know your lie-bashers love you and are doing this for your own good. A spouse and an accountability partner are good candidates.

Second, you need to ask God for His help on a regular basis, whether you feel like it or not. A small or next-to-nothing faith will suffice, and don't let the size of your faith stop you from praying. God will still hear you. When you pray for God's assistance, He'll give it to you (Matthew 18:19). One of your main weapons in this spiritual war against Satan is prayer. As it says in Ephesians 6:18, "With all prayer and petition pray at all times in the Spirit." Pray on your own. Pray with your spouse. Pray with your accountability partner. Pray that God will use this process to get Satan's lies out of your mind and your heavenly Father's truths in.

Third, read the Bible regularly whether you feel like it or not. The Bible is the main source of God's truth. The sword of the Spirit is one of your main weapons in this spiritual war (Ephesians 6:17). God will bless you for reading His Word and will lead you to the specific truths He wants inserted in your mind.

Attack and Replace

It was time to show my depressed client how to attack her lies and replace them with God's truth. I'll illustrate how I did this by using the examples in chapter 9:

Client's core lie: I'm not pretty.

Me: If you're that ugly, you really ought to put a bag over your head. That way you won't frighten people. Who would have married such a troll? Did you marry a blind man? Oh, you didn't? Who taught you that you weren't pretty?

It was your dad, wasn't it? It was his job to make you feel attractive, and he blew it. He was clueless, and he was wrong!

The truth is, you are attractive. Your husband thinks you're beautiful, doesn't he? He's either a liar, or you are beautiful. God made you, and He thinks you're beautiful. Read and meditate on Psalm 139:13–16.

Client's core lie: I'm stupid.

Me: Forgetting something doesn't mean you're stupid. It means you forgot something. That's all. Everybody, even rocket scientists and Nobel Prize winners, have an occasional lapse of memory.

Did you graduate from high school? You did? Did you graduate from college? You did? Have you held this job for five years? You have? Do you take care of the kids, help with their homework, cook meals, and run your home? You do? It amazes me how a stupid person such as yourself can do all these things! If I didn't know better, I'd say you were intelligent.

I'm impressed that you can read minds. You know what your boss is thinking! No, you don't! You're guessing. Of course, your guesses are all negative and irrational. What a surprise! It's as if your boss said to your face: "You're stupid! You're incompetent! You're an airhead! I can't trust you! One more mistake and you're fired!" He said none of those things! The truth is that he wasn't that upset.

The truth is that you are a bright and competent

person who makes an occasional mistake. God has given you a spiritual gift, so He obviously thinks you're smart enough to use it to advance His kingdom.

Client's core lie: I can't make good, close friends.

Me: Let's see. I wonder why you didn't click with any ladies at the party? You got there late. You didn't play any of the games. You decided you were uninteresting. You didn't sign up for any Bible studies.

Do you see what happened? You sabotaged yourself! You could make close friends, but you don't want to. You're scared of rejection. It's easier and safer to hide behind the lie that you can't make friends. It's also lonely and miserable, but that's your choice.

I guess your husband is attracted to uninteresting women. Lucky for you! Because the truth is, you are an interesting person who can make good, close friends. Your husband is your close friend. Your accountability partner is your close friend. Ask them what they think about you. Then believe it.

God wants you to have friends. He instructs you to be in church with others and to help others through difficult times. How can you do these things without developing close friends?

Now it was my client's turn to practice the attack-and-replace process. I asked her to study one of her core lies and use her new skills to shred it and replace it with God's truth.

Her core lie: I must stuff all difficult emotions, especially anger.

Her response: I hide behind my belief that I'm only hurt.
Actually I was angry at my husband for what he
said. I don't care if he meant it or not. I was angry!
I call myself a peacemaker. That sounds so noble.
Too bad it's a lie. I'm a wimp! I let others, even
my dear husband, walk on me and I say nothing!
I stuff my feelings and stay depressed. By saying
nothing to my husband, I'm lying to him. I end
up hurting him and the kids with my smoldering resentments and depression. The truth is that
I was angry, and it's okay to be angry. Ephesians
4:25 says I need to speak truth to others.
Ephesians 4:26–27 says it's okay to be angry, and
it's my responsibility to express my anger directly
with the person before the end of the day.

It took my client about a month to get the hang of this
attack-and-replace process. Her husband, her accountability
partner, and I challenged her lies and spoke God's truth to her
over and over. Eventually she could do it for herself.

Flushing out her lies and holding to God's truths took a
big bite out of her depressive lifestyle. She began feeling less
depressed, more confident, and more hopeful.

The Four Columns
To further solidify her skill in the attack-and-replace process, I
had my client use a modified version of my three-column writing technique by adding a fourth column. The extra column is
headed by the question *What was the truth?* Writing down the
truth helps it become more firmly embedded in her new mind.

Using the same three-column examples from chapter 9, here's what my client came up with:

What happened?	What did you think and feel?	What was the truth?	What was the result?
I forgot to show up at my son's school fundraiser.

I had volunteered, but it slipped my mind.

My son was disappointed.

I got an e-mail from the volunteer coordinator saying, "Where were you?" | I felt embarrassed and angry at myself.

I'm stupid, irresponsible, and a bad mom (lies). | I made a mistake. That's all there is to it.

I was embarrassed and angry, but I don't have to stay that way.

This mistake doesn't make me stupid, irresponsible, or a bad mom.

I am bright.

I am responsible most of the time.

I am a good mom—not perfect, but good.

God created me (Psalm 139:13–16) and He loves me (John 3:16). | I felt bad for a few hours, but then I got over it.

I apologized to my son, and he was okay with it.

I called the volunteer coordinator and said sorry, I had simply forgotten. |

What happened?	What did you think and feel?	What was the truth?	What was the result?
I heard a sermon Sunday on the evils of abortion. The pastor made it clear abortion is the murder of an innocent child.	I was devastated, felt horribly guilty, and cried all during the sermon. I killed someone and can't be forgiven (the second part is a lie). I'm a bad person (a lie). God is still punishing me for my abortion (a lie). I deserve to be depressed (a lie).	I did feel devastated and guilty, but I can express and release those feelings. God has completely forgiven me (Romans 5:8). God has removed my sins far from me (Psalm 103:12). I am a sinner, but God loves me dearly (John 3:16). God wants me to be joyful and to live a peaceful and abundant life (John 15:11, 14:27, 10:10).	I felt depressed for the afternoon. I talked out my pain with my husband and accountability partner. I prayed with my husband for God's comfort and peace. I read John 15:11, 14:27, 10:10 and meditated on these verses. I will always regret the abortion, but I can move ahead in God's strength.

You will notice that the first two columns were the same, but the last two columns are quite different. Because she refuted her lies and inserted God's truths, she felt better. Healthier. Stronger. She was able to stop the damage her lies were doing to her life.

Create a Card Catalog
Look at the *What was the truth?* column my client wrote concerning the pastor's sermon and her abortion. She wrote down each verse on a three-by-five card. Because of the number of verses, she used the front and the back of the card.

When Satan attacked her with lies about her abortion, she counterattacked by getting out that particular card and reading and meditating on the verses. She was doing what Jesus did to combat Satan and his lies in Matthew 4. Satan had used lies about her abortion for years to keep her guilty and depressed. He still tried, but she was ready with God's Word to get rid of him and his lies.

She developed cards with verses for all her core lies. Although she continued to use her cards as a reference, she got to the point where she could recall the needed verses in her head.

After several months of using the attack-and-replace techniques, my client was thinking more accurately and biblically. Increasingly, she could actually defeat her lies and insert God's truth at the time of the event. Not always, but sometimes. She was still depressed, but she was making progress.

To aid you in the truth-replacement process, develop a list of specific verses to counter your specific core lies. Write these verses on three-by-five cards and keep them handy. When certain core lies pop up, go to your card catalog and pull out the verse card that counters those lies. This is a practical and powerful use of the sword of the Spirit (Ephesians 6:17).

Do Your Work

1. Read 2 Corinthians 10:5 and meditate on it. Ask God to help you "take every thought captive to the obedience of Christ."

2. Commit—right now—to regularly pray and read the Bible. Do it no matter where you are in your relationship with God. Ask someone close to you to hold you accountable in these two vital areas.

3. Ask a support team member to read this chapter. Ask them to attack your lies out loud to you and give you God's truths when you describe events to them.

4. Practice talking through the attack-and-replace system on your own.

5. Practice the four-column technique for two weeks. Share what you write with your support team members.

6. Develop a card catalog of verses to counter your core lies.

CHAPTER 11

GOD DIDN'T MAKE ROBOTS: TO HEAL, YOU MUST EXPRESS YOUR EMOTIONS

You'll take a big chunk out of your emotional problem by correcting your thinking. But you've got more work to do. The next step in your journey to emotional health is learning how to express your emotions in a healthy way.

Thinking and emotion are intimately connected, and so both must be addressed in your healing. Growing up, you experienced some painful, traumatic events. In these traumatic events, distorted thinking and damaged emotions were fused together. To be truly emotionally healthy, you must learn to do two things:

- Think accurately and biblically.

- Identify and express your emotions in a healthy way.

A Revealing List
I will now conduct a brief self-awareness exercise. Psychologists love tests because they can tell us important information about a person. My exercise is a variation of the word-association test, the one in which the psychologist says a word and the person being tested says the first word that comes into his or her head:

- I say *boy*. You say *girl*.

- I say *fruit*. You say *banana*.

- I say *breath*. You say *bad*.

My exercise is based on the six statements written below. After reading each statement, I want you to close your eyes for ten or fifteen seconds and notice your internal reaction to the statement. Use your imagination. Let your mind go. Put yourself in the situation. Then open your eyes and follow the same procedure for the next statement.

- You are walking into your first-grade classroom on the first day of school.

- That person you really wanted to date has just made it clear that the attraction is not mutual.

- You've just been married and you're leaving on your honeymoon.

- Someone you love has just been diagnosed with a terminal illness.

- Your car has broken down fifty miles east of Gallup, New Mexico, in the middle of the desert.

- You are on a deserted beach watching the sunset with the person you love most in the world.

We Are Emotional Creatures
These six events trigger emotions, don't they? My point with this little test is to show that we're emotional creatures.

- fear

- rejection

- anger

- depression

- exhilaration

- joy

- love

- peace

Of course, this is my made-up list. If I knew you, if I knew what had happened in your life this past year or month or week, I could come up with a list of six specific, targeted events that would trigger you emotionally in some powerful ways:

- job stress;

- great vacation;

- marital problems;

- birth of a child;

- physical illness;

- God working in your life.

We are designed by God to respond to events in our lives with emotions.

Emotions in the Bible

The Bible is full of evidence that God made us to be emotional creatures. From Adam and Eve in Genesis to John, the author of Revelation, hundreds of biblical personalities expressed emotions of every kind and at many different levels of intensity. Just like you, and just like me.

Let me briefly highlight the emotional life of one person: Jesus Christ.

Jesus Christ, the perfect God-man, had a rich emotional life during His time on earth. Even a cursory reading of the Gospels reveals a Person who experienced and expressed the entire gamut of emotions. He expressed them openly and freely and without apology—to His heavenly Father and the humans He had contact with.

Here's an overview of just some of the emotions Jesus felt and expressed during His three-year ministry:

- Anxiety: Luke 22:41–44

- Grief: Luke 19:41–44; John 11:32–44; Hebrews 5:7

- Anger: Mark 3:5, 10:14, 11:15–17

- Joy: Luke 10:21–24

- Frustration: Mark 9:19

- Disappointment: Mark 8:12

- Compassion: Mark 1:41

Jesus is God. In His incarnation (when He lived as a human being on Earth), He was emotionally and spiritually the healthiest person who ever walked the earth. He is our central example in life (Ephesians 5:1–2; Philippians 2:5–8). Therefore we ought to seek to share our emotions as He shared His.

Our Brains Are Wired Emotionally

Years ago, two brain surgeons decided to try an experiment with a number of their patients during brain surgery. Using electrodes, they stimulated parts of their patients' brains.

What they discovered was fascinating. When certain parts of the brains were stimulated, the patients spontaneously shared memories and emotions. It was as if they were living these events all over again with all the details and all the emotions. Some of these events were thirty years in the past. Others had occurred in the week before surgery.

What does this mean? First, we are all wired emotionally. That's how God made us. Second, it's never too late to start learning how to express emotions. The emotions and the events they are connected to are all stored in the brain.

The Definition of an Emotion

An emotion is a temporary, automatic, internal reaction to an event of perceived personal significance.

- *Temporary:* A warning bell that something of personal importance has happened. Not necessarily brief, but designed to alert you to the event and begin the process of dealing with it.

- *Automatic:* A reflex. No choice is involved. Emotions are not right or wrong, although thinking and behavior can be wrong. Emotions are just reactions.

- *Internal:* Emotions happen inside a person.

- *An event of perceived personal significance:* The event can be good or bad, but it's meaningful to you. If you perceive the event to be personally significant, then you respond with an emotion. Depending on the event, the emotion can be intense or barely noticeable. Factors that can increase the intensity and duration of an emotion are your stress level, if your needs are being met, and if the event triggers your past unresolved pain.

The Purpose of Emotions

Emotions serve a three-fold purpose:

- *To reveal self:* Emotions are windows into who you are inside. They expose your thoughts, your values, your needs, and your view of life and relationships.

- *To keep your emotional system running smoothly:* Expressing your emotions in the right way leads to a healthy frame of mind and prevents depression, anxiety, addictions, and other emotional health problems.

- *To build genuine intimacy in relationships:* Emotional expression is a huge part of how you connect to God and others. Can you imagine love without emotion? Passion without emotion? Playfulness without emotion? A stimulating conversation without emotion? Resolving conflict without emotion? Worship without emotion?

Express Your Significant Emotions in Four Ways

If you want to be emotionally healthy and create intimacy in your relationships, you must learn how to express your significant emotions in four ways.

You don't express all of your emotions. There simply isn't time. You have thousands every day. You'd have to quit your job and just sit around all day emoting. An emotion is significant if the feeling is intense, if it lingers for several hours, or if it affects an important relationship. Then it needs to be expressed. If in doubt, express it. Better safe than sorry.

I'm talking about positive *and* difficult emotions. It can be just as hard to express love as it is to express anger. Ephesians 4:15

contains a guiding principle about the expression of emotions: Speak the truth in love. You must get the emotion out and do it in as loving a way as possible.

Here are the four ways you need to express your emotions:

Immediately

Express the emotion as soon as possible after the event.

Plan A is right when the event happens and you feel the emotion. The exception is when you are intensely angry. Take some time to simmer down. You can't do a good job communicating anger when you're in a rage. No one can. Don't do it, at least not yet. Wait awhile. You'll still be angry, but much more in control.

Plan B is to express the emotion as soon as humanly possible. The sooner you express your emotion, the sooner it's out of you and you can avoid its damaging effects.

Any significant emotion—positive or difficult—will do damage to you and the relationship if it's not expressed. Love and passion not expressed will weaken a relationship and, in so doing, harm you. As we saw in the two previous chapters with my depressed client, anger and other negative emotions will fuel depression and misery if held inside.

Ephesians 4:26 commands us to express anger before the sun goes down. This is a good principle for all emotions. Get them out before the end of the day. We're not designed by God to hold in emotions. We're designed to release them.

If you delay beyond a day, you're stalling. You may never express it. Additionally your stuffed emotions build in intensity over time and cause increasing damage to you and the relationship. Anger expressed a week later is a whole lot worse than anger expressed the same day.

Spontaneously

Express emotion in a natural, unrestrained style. Think of it as an instinctive reaction. It's not forced or planned. Your emotion comes up, and you release it through your spoken words.

If you feel love for your wife, tell her! Tell her right when you feel it. That way, it's fresh and packs a punch. If you're at work, call her or e-mail her. If you're in her presence, tell her to her face. If you don't tell her spontaneously, something electric and vibrant is lost. Plus, there's a reasonable chance you'll forget.

Directly

Express your emotion directly to the person it's connected with. Here's an emotional fact: Unless your emotion is expressed directly, it is not released, and the relationship is damaged. The one exception is if the object of your anger or other difficult emotion would have a violent reaction and physically harm you or kill you. If a member of Hell's Angels scrapes your car as he pulls his Harley out of the parking lot, don't track him down and express your anger. In this case, you can vent your anger about Harley Man with someone close to you.

My daughter, Nancy, is known for her ability to express her emotions directly. She's to the point and doesn't waste time on the frills. On her first day in kindergarten, one unfortunate boy decided to throw sand in her face. Nancy promptly threw sand back in his face and said, "Throwing sand in my face makes me angry." He cried his little eyes out, and Nancy told us later: "The punk deserved it." He didn't bother her again.

Recently, I took three of my kids to dinner because Sandy was out of town. Emily and William were in the backseat. I was in the front with Nancy, who was driving. She has her restricted driving permit. Nancy, who knows no fear on the road, was accelerating up to a line of stopped cars. Here's our dialogue:

Me: Brake, Nancy, brake! Those cars are stopped!

Nancy: I know. I'm not blind.

Me: Honey, my job is to teach you how to drive.

Nancy (without missing a beat): No, your job is to keep me
          from killing us. I get frustrated when you
          point out the obvious.

Emily and William: Let us out! Stop the car! She's going to
          kill us! We want to live!

Nancy, although she needs to work on the "in love" part
of Ephesians 4:15, is a good example of how to express your
emotions directly. Her directness in emotional expression makes
her assertive and protects her from being disrespected and
mistreated.

Scripture teaches us to deal directly. As we saw in chapter
10, Jesus Christ spoke directly to His disciples, to the religious
leaders, and to everyone He came into contact with. Paul was
also a direct person. He was clear in his dealings with friends,
supporters, the religious leaders, and the churches to whom
he wrote. Ephesians 4:15–32 and Colossians 3:8–17 teach
us to speak truth to one another. Matthew 5:23–24 instructs
a person to immediately leave the church altar if he realizes
there's something between him and a brother in Christ. Where
do you go? To that brother to seek to be reconciled. Deal
directly.

Fully

Make sure you get all your emotion out. Don't downplay or short-circuit the process. If the event is traumatic—the death of a loved one, an affair, a divorce, the loss of a job, abuse—the process of fully expressing will take time and be intense. Full expression of the emotions connected to a serious trauma will take months.

In a marriage relationship or close friendship, it takes time to get all your emotions out. This is true for difficult as well as positive emotions. All great conversations involve emotions and take place in stages. Over the course of a few hours or a few days, the partners keep revisiting the same issues and expressing their emotions.

I have focused on difficult emotions because they are a lot tougher to express. But you need to follow the four guidelines above in the expression of *all* your significant emotions.

Identify and Express Emotions

My depressed client had made good progress attacking her distorted thoughts—her lies—and replacing them with God's truth. Now she needed to learn how to express her emotions in the four ways I just described. Her poor expression of emotions was also feeding her depression and crippling her important relationships.

The first step was having her describe events—and her emotions connected to those events—to me, her husband, and her accountability partner. Her job was to answer three questions about each event:

1. What were my emotions?

2. What did I do with my emotions?

3. What was the impact on me and on the relationship?

She discovered that she handled her emotions poorly. She stuffed them, and she did not express them to anyone. The impact was more depression and no closeness in any of her relationships.

One event involved her boss, who had made a sarcastic, cutting comment to her about her work. She was angry and hurt but kept these emotions inside. She felt victimized, depressed, and resentful.

Expressing these emotions to her husband and accountability partner helped her gain some release and relief. A week later, she was able to tell her boss how she felt about his comment. Even though his response was not compassionate and understanding, dealing directly with him was a huge step forward for her. She released her emotions and felt a surge of self-respect and confidence.

A Daily Emotional Journal

Since my client had been using the three- and four-column techniques I explained in chapter 9, she had already begun to identify her emotions. To focus on her emotions and their impact on her life, I asked her to use four columns and answer these questions (modified slightly from the previously described four-column questions):

1. What happened?

2. What did you feel?

3. What did you do with your emotions?

4. What was the result?

Here are a few of the events she assessed over a two-week period:

- Her husband made a crude comment to her in front of friends.

- Her daughter created a scene at the grocery store.

- She saw a movie, and it brought back positive emotions about a week at camp in junior high.

- God spoke to her and touched her through a Bible study at church.

- A friend's mother died.

Doing the four columns on each of these events gave her a good picture of her emotions, how she stuffed them, and the negative impact stuffing them had on her life and relationships. She used this tool to begin expressing her emotions in healthier ways.

Eventually, she used the four-column approach to learn to correctly express her emotions and think in an accurate, biblical way.

No one is born with the ability to express emotions spontaneously, immediately, directly, and fully. As you experience pain, you and your sin nature develop unhealthy, damaging ways of dealing with your emotions. With time, practice, and the power of God you will learn how to express emotions consistently with your new nature in Christ.

Do Your Work

1. How were emotions expressed in your home? How did your dad express emotions? How did your mom express them? What did your parents teach you or model for you about emotional expression?

2. Recall three events in your life that involved intense emotions, either positive or difficult. Describe what happened, the emotions you felt, what you did with your emotions, and the impact on your life.

3. Rate yourself in the four healthy ways of expressing emotions: spontaneously, immediately, directly, and fully. In which of these areas do you struggle? Which emotions are the most challenging for you to express in these ways?

4 Ask a support team member to read this chapter. Then, describe daily events to them using these three questions: What were my emotions? What did I do with my emotions? What was the impact on me and the relationship?

5. Keep an emotional journal (four-columns) every day for two weeks. Share your journal with a support team member.

CHAPTER 12

IT'S OKAY TO BE ANGRY:
YOU CAN STUFF IT, SPEW IT,
OR EXPRESS IT IN A HEALTHY WAY

Several years ago, I was sitting in my office talking with a client. I have a huge picture window that reveals the entire rear two hundred feet of my property. It's a peaceful, pastoral scene with towering oak trees. Suddenly in the middle of this morning session with a client, a chicken came around the corner of my building and began pecking and rooting in my flower bed just outside my big window. The chicken was making a mess of my pristine flower bed.

It was strange and distracting. My client and I laughed about the chicken and finished the session. I went outside and gently shooed the chicken away. I thought that was the end of my relationship with the chicken. I was wrong.

During my next session, the chicken returned and resumed rooting in my flower bed. That's when I felt the first stirrings of anger. Who did this chicken think it was? Where did it come from? Why had it chosen my flower bed to systematically destroy? I pasted on a smile for my client and forced my anger down. It wouldn't be professional to rant and rave about the chicken in front of a client. After all, I was a man of dignity and self-control who could certainly maintain his emotional composure.

That stupid chicken would not leave me alone. Maybe it thought I was its mother! Over the next week, I shooed it away ten times a day, but it always came back. That chicken was threatening my peace of mind and my ability to concentrate.

During my therapy sessions, I could hear it clucking and scratching. I'm still proud that I controlled my anger for a week.

But after one week, I lost it. I became openly furious with that chicken. I raised my voice when I shooed it away. All right, I yelled at it. "Chicken, get out of my flower bed and my life! This is not your home! I'm not your mommy! If you don't leave, I'm going to drop you off at the nearest Kentucky Fried Chicken restaurant! Do you understand me?" The chicken just ignored me and kept coming back.

A terrible realization dawned on me a week and a half into this battle: The chicken must die. I mulled over various methods of execution: poison, a baseball bat, a big rock, or wringing its neck. But all these were messy. I decided the best way was to simply run the chicken over with my car. I could then bury the chicken—in an unmarked grave—at the back of my property.

One Saturday, when no one was around, I shooed the chicken out into the middle of my backyard. I gunned the engine of my small sedan and hurtled toward the doomed chicken. When I was only ten yards away, the chicken looked up. I thought I saw disappointment in its beady little chicken eyes.

Surprisingly, I couldn't kill the chicken with my car, but not from lack of trying. That chicken was too quick. Four times I made a run at it, and four times it nimbly skipped out of the way just before impact. That chicken refused to die! I could picture myself in a rubber room in a mental hospital, and that chicken would still be rooting in my flower bed!

Sandy came up with the solution: Ask Denise Hall, a good friend with a love for animals who lived out in the boonies, to come and get the chicken. My first reaction was, "No! That chicken doesn't deserve to live a pampered life! It's going to die, and I'm going to be there to see it!" But I recovered my composure and followed Sandy's advice. My nightmare was over.

Several months after Denise took the chicken home, it disappeared. I panicked, sure that the chicken was going to find some way to come back to my flower bed. But I've never seen it again.

My chicken story is a silly way of illustrating how anger operates. My family, friends, and I had some great laughs over my week and a half battle with the bird. Anger is not funny, however, when it happens in relationships with other humans. It can do incredible damage to you and your relationships.

Unresolved or poorly expressed anger is a main source of many emotional, physical, and spiritual problems. It's crippling and kills relationships. Handled improperly, anger can be a hugely destructive force. Handled properly, the way God wants you to handle it, anger can be a positive, constructive, and healing force.

To become emotionally healthy, you must learn how to express your anger in a biblically accurate and psychologically sound way.

Definition of Anger

Anger is a temporary, automatic emotional and physiological reaction to a perceived threat to needs. When something happens that you perceive to be a threat—to your self-image, needs, way of life, dignity, values, and beliefs—you will feel angry.

It can be the *threat* of loss: A loved one becomes ill, a job is in jeopardy, or a child may be planning to leave for college. It can be an *actual* loss: The loved one dies, the job is lost, your child does leave for college. Or it can be change. Change, positive or negative, equals loss.

Your perception of the threat can be right or wrong. If a

loved one dies, that's obviously a real loss. If you misinterpret your spouse's statement, that would be a false threat. But either way, you will still feel angry.

Everybody Gets Angry

Anger is an integral part of the emotional makeup of all human beings. It's a healthy, normal emotion. It's part of the standard equipment for human personality, straight from God, the manufacturer.

Scripture supports the fact that anger is part of the human experience. God was angry (Exodus 4:14) and Jesus, as we saw in the previous chapter, expressed anger. We can infer that many righteous, God-fearing individuals in the Bible got angry: Moses (Exodus 32:19–28), David (Psalm 31:17–18), Elijah (1 Kings 18:21–40), Nehemiah (Nehemiah 4:4–5, 5:1–13), Job (Job 10:1–7, 16:1–6), and Paul (Acts 15:36–40; 1 Corinthians 5:1–13; Galatians 2:11–14).

How Anger Operates

Anger is an automatic reaction to a perceived threat. More specifically, anger is an early warning system. Pain means something's wrong in the body. Anger means something's wrong in a relationship.

Anger is the gateway emotion, which means it is the first step in a chain of emotional expression. Here's how the chain works:

Threat: loss or fear of loss;

Anger: a temporary reaction to the threat;

Hurt: pain, depression, grief, disappointment, anxiety;

Love: for self, others, and God; intimacy, connection, needs met, hurts forgiven, reconciliation.

Anger begins the emotional process of dealing with the threat. It helps you mobilize and prepare to face the threat. If you can't express your anger in the right way, you can't fully express the other important emotions that follow. Poorly expressed anger will block your entire emotional system and cause all kinds of emotional, physical, and spiritual problems.

Keep in mind, anger is temporary and not to be confused with aggression or hostility:

- *Aggression:* a destructive behavioral act when anger is violently released.

- *Hostility:* a smoldering resentment and bitterness when anger is held in.

Get Rid of Anger

So, you experience anger. I experience anger. We all experience anger. What do we do with it? Scripture is crystal clear: Anger, whether it stems from a righteous or sinful source, must be cleaned out of the emotional system as soon as possible. In Ephesians 4:25–27, Paul provides some very specific teaching about anger: "Therefore, laying aside falsehood, speak truth each one of you with his neighbor, for we are members of one another. Be angry, and yet do not sin; do not let the sun go down on your anger, and do not give the devil an opportunity."

Seven critical points can be drawn from this passage:

1. Speak the truth directly with others.

2. Sometimes that truth will be anger.

3. It's okay to be angry.

4. You can get rid of anger without sinning.

5. You need to express your anger before the day ends.

6. You need to express your anger directly with others.

7. If you don't express your anger correctly, you will give Satan "an opportunity."

The anger Paul describes in Ephesians 4:26 is not sinful anger. It's not rage or hostility, but the anger that precedes rage and hostility. If you express this anger, it is released, and you won't sin.

The anger mentioned in Ephesians 4:31 is an entirely different kind of anger: "Let all bitterness and wrath and anger and clamor and slander be put away from you, along with all malice." The terms in this verse refer to anger that is sinful and destructive: smoldering, held-in resentments and explosive, violent wrath.

I believe Paul is saying that if you don't express your Ephesians 4:26 anger, you'll end up with Ephesians 4:31 anger. And that kind of anger breaks God's law and destroys you. It will also prevent you from experiencing Ephesians 4:32 (which immediately follows Paul's teaching about anger): "Be kind to one another, tender-hearted, forgiving each other, just as God in Christ also has forgiven you."

I'm convinced Paul is talking about *significant anger* in this Ephesians passage. You don't need to express anger about every little frustration or annoyance. "Love covers a multitude of sins" (1 Peter 4:8); use love in this way. Your anger is significant if it is intense, lingers for several hours, or affects a relationship.

There are three ways to deal with your anger. Read these

three options, and I'll bet you'll recognize yourself. If you don't, ask your spouse or accountability partner. One of them will know how you handle anger.

Stuff It

Stuffers suppress anger, deny it, ignore it, and pretend it isn't there. They hold anger in. They try to protect themselves and avoid dealing with conflict by clamming up. It's a powerful tool, because no one can make a stuffer talk. They control with silence.

Stuffing is sin (Ephesians 4:31; Hebrews 12:15) and leads to bitterness, resentment, hostility, and hatred. Not because you want it to. It just does. Stuffing is also lying because the stuffer is angry and isn't saying so.

Stuffers are masters at denial. They say they're not angry, even when the whole neighborhood knows they are:

Spouse: Honey, what's wrong?

Stuffer: Nothing.

Spouse: Honey, really, I think you're upset. You broke our bedroom door off the hinges, and you haven't talked to me for two hours. What's wrong?

Stuffer (teeth clenched, neck veins throbbing): I said nothing's wrong.

Spouse: You're angry, aren't you?

Stuffer: I am not angry!

Even if stuffers admit they're angry, they won't talk about it. They might say, "All right, I am angry. That's right. And I've got some pretty good reasons to be. But I won't tell you what they are because *I don't want to talk about it.*"

Stuffers hate conflict and will do anything to avoid it. They'd rather take a beating than face a conflict. They'll deny. They'll say nothing. They'll change the subject. They'll use humor to avoid sensitive issues. If all else fails, they'll walk away. They'll go to another room or leave in the car. All a spouse will hear is running feet and the car starting.

Here are some classic stuffer styles:

The pouter. Pouters won't deal directly with another person. They'll slink off and pout, sometimes for days. They think, *I'm going to make you suffer. I'm going to punish you with the silent treatment.*

The crier. The crier tries to bypass anger by feeling hurt. "I'm not angry, I'm just hurt." They feel sad and sorry for themselves. They cry on the inside and maybe on the outside until the other person goes away or feels sorry for them.

The denier. With a smile, they say: "Me, angry? Oh no, not at all. I'm fine." Liar! Faker! They've gotten Oscars for their denial performances. If they say they're not angry, then they believe there's no problem that has to be addressed.

There are three results of stuffing anger:

The anger remains and intensifies. It's like stuffing dirty clothes in the back of the closet. No one can see them, but they're still there, and they smell.

Personal damage is done. Stuffing leads to a variety of emotional, physical, and spiritual problems. Stuffing is a tremendous drain on the stuffer's energy. They will almost certainly die young. When the casket and burial plot salesmen call, stuffers had better buy. Their tombstone can have these words etched on it: THIS DEAR SOUL DIED YOUNG BUT NEVER EXPRESSED ANGER.

Relationship damage is done. Stuffing destroys relationships with others and with God. Conflicts will not be resolved. Stuffers will not be able to forgive. There is no depth or intimacy in relationships unless anger is shared in a healthy way. Stuffing equals superficial relationships.

The solution for stuffers is to learn how to speak up and tell the truth about feelings. They have to work hard at identifying and expressing anger.

Spew It

Spewers blow anger out forcibly. They verbally and sometimes physically explode. They don't hold back. They lash out. Spewing is a powerful tool because you can't make a spewer shut up. They control with speaking.

Spewing is sin. Read the third chapter of James and what it says about the tongue. The most deadly weapon on earth is not the nuclear warhead. It's the tongue.

Spewers suffer from these four problems:

- *Overexpression.* They talk too much.

- *High volume.* They yell and scream. They may not realize they're yelling, but everyone else knows.

- *Critical tone.* They personally attack other people's character. They fight dirty.

- *Woodpecker syndrome.* They'll follow their spouses all over the house, pecking at them. They are incredible pests! They are like a woodpecker fused to the forehead. "Let's talk. We have to talk. Can you hear me in there?"

Spewers have the sensitivity of a baby's behind. They are irritable and touchy. It doesn't take much to anger spewers. "You didn't close the front door again. I knew you couldn't be trusted." They suddenly become furious, like a tornado coming out of nowhere.

Spewers have the memory of an elephant. They remember every mistake and every hurt from the beginning of every relationship. They'll bring up the past when they're angry. "May 10, 1990. Remember that date? I'll bet you don't. Ten p.m. and I was in the bathroom. You failed to replace the toilet paper roll. I was stranded. I'll never forget that!"

The three results of spewing anger are the same as stuffing it:

- The anger remains and intensifies.

- Personal damage is done.

- Relationship damage is done.

The solution for spewers is to learn how to tone down anger. Use fewer words. Work on the love part of speaking the truth in love. Be more gentle. Take the edge off.

It's quite common for a stuffer to occasionally turn into a spewer. They stuff and stuff and stuff and finally blow. They spew all their anger in one big torrent of words. Then they go back to stuffing again.

I have some helpful hints for those of you who are married.

Think of this as a public service. If you are not willing to express your anger correctly, then here are some ways to get back at your partner:

- *Wives:* Make sure the house is a mess. Talk to your parents and friends about your husband's shortcomings. Nag your husband constantly. Deny him sex or endure it as duty. Spend as much money as you can.

- *Husbands:* Withdraw into silence. Work long hours and come home late. Treat your children harshly. Become critical of your wife's looks, housekeeping skills, and mothering abilities. Read your wife the submission passages in scripture.

These are all ways that anger is expressed. Actually, you don't need me to point these out. If you're not dealing with anger the right way, you're already doing these behaviors, aren't you? You have to! You're forced to! You're giving the devil all kinds of opportunities. If you let him, Satan will use your incorrectly expressed anger every time.

Express It

The only way to appropriately release significant anger is to express it verbally using correct communication principles. This is the only way to obey Ephesians 4:26 and get rid of anger without sinning. Of course, this is also the most difficult way.

It makes no difference if your anger stems from a sinful or incorrect perception. Who cares if the other person didn't mean to threaten and anger you? You're still angry, and it won't go away. What does the Bible tell you to do with your sin? Confess it (James 5:16).

There are three results of expressing anger:

- *The anger is released.* It's gone.

- *Personal health is improved.* Since anger is designed by God to be only temporary, when you express it correctly your emotional system can run smoothly. With your anger out, you can identify and express the important emotions that lie underneath. Your emotional, physical, and spiritual health will all improve.

- *Relationships are improved.* Your relationships with others and God improve. Conflicts can be resolved. Forgiveness can take place. Real intimacy and passion and depth can happen.

How to Express Anger in a Healthy Way

Ask God for help
You can't express anger in the right way in your own power. It's a supernatural job, as is the healthy expression of all emotions. Ask God, through the Holy Spirit, to help you in this process. Even if your faith is weak, He'll give you the power and courage you need.

Identify and express your significant anger
My depressed client had made good progress identifying and expressing her emotions, but anger was her biggest challenge. She would often deny being angry and say, "I'm not angry. I'm just hurt."

I would always respond, "Baloney. Where there's hurt, there's anger. If you stay stuck in your hurt feelings, you'll stay depressed." Quite often, I'd tell her, "The only people you can express your anger with are your kids. You can keep beating up on them with your words, or you can learn to express your anger directly to those you are angry with."

With the help of her husband and accountability partner, my client used the retelling of events and the emotional journal to practice identifying and expressing her anger. If her anger was significant (intense, lasted several hours, or affected a relationship), she would practice expressing it to her husband and accountability partner. She would often pretend that these support team members were people she was angry with. She was preparing to deal directly with those people her anger was connected with.

Take anger to God and to the source
After practicing the expression of her anger, my client would pray and then go to the person she was angry with and release her anger directly. Tough? No question about it. Biblical? Read Jesus' words in Matthew 5:23–24 and the answer will be clear: " 'Therefore if you are presenting your offering at the altar, and there remember that your brother has something against you, leave your offering there before the altar and go; first be reconciled to your brother, and then come and present your offering.' "

You are to go and deal directly *regardless of the other person's reaction*. A negative reaction from the other person is no excuse to avoid the confrontation. Jesus says to go to the person. There are no exceptions in this passage. When you go, you clean out your anger, obey God, and create the possibility of reconciliation.

Speak the truth in love
Be honest, be brief, and be specific. Don't sugarcoat the issue

or water it down. Speak truth, firmly but as kindly as possible. Your first four words need to be: "I am angry because. . ." Just do your part and don't worry about the other person's reaction. You are working on your half of the bridge of reconciliation. The other half is the other person's responsibility.

Express anger as quickly as possible
As we read in Ephesians 4:26, get your anger out before the end of the day.

Give yourself time to learn
If you're new at expressing anger, you'll make plenty of mistakes. It will be messy for a while as you learn this skill. Warn those close to you that you're working on expressing your anger. Practice with small, trivial situations so you can get the hang of it.

Past, Unresolved Anger
It's possible—almost a certainty in fact—that you have a backlog of unexpressed anger. Bitterness and resentment are percolating inside and transferring to your close relationships in the present day.

This was true of my depressed client. She had filed away anger for years, and she had a warehouse full of it. Learning to express her day-to-day anger in the present helped her to a degree. Her emotional system began running more smoothly, and her depression did improve. It was time for her to use her skills to face her unresolved pain from the past.

Do Your Work

1. What have you been taught—by parents, your church, Christian media, books—about anger and its expression? Compare what you have been taught to the truths communicated in Ephesians 4:25–27.

2. Of the seven critical points drawn from Ephesians 4:25–27, which ones do you struggle with the most?

3. What do you get angry about? Which situations or people trigger your anger the most?

4. Do you stuff your anger or spew it? Tell a support team member about one recent episode and how you handled your anger.

5. What damage, to you and your relationships, is your anger causing?

6. With the help of a support team member, practice identifying and expressing your anger using retelling and the daily emotional journal. Follow the six guidelines provided at the end of this chapter.

7. What past, unresolved anger do you have? Who are you still angry with? How does this unresolved anger impact your life and relationships today?

CHAPTER 13

WONDER WOMAN YOU'RE NOT: HOW TO STOP BEING A STRESS QUEEN

Kate is a woman. In fact, she's Wonder Woman. She does it all!

- Who keeps the home clean? She does. Who vacuums and scrubs the toilets and tubs and sinks? She does. Who picks up the shoes, the clothes, the glasses, the toys, and the candy bar wrappers left out by the people who live with her? She does. Who does the laundry? She does. Who does the grocery shopping? She does. Who cooks most of the meals? She does. Who buys most of the things needed in the home? She does.

- Who does most of the child rearing? She does. Who wipes the kids' noses, takes care of them when they're sick, bathes them, dresses them, plays with them, prays with them, and disciplines them? She does. Who cleans up their constant messes? She does. Who changes ninety-five percent of their disgusting, poop-filled diapers? Her husband. Yeah, right. She does. Who drops them off at the bus stop, takes them to school, or homeschools them? She does. Who helps them with their homework? She does. Who carts them to all their activities? She does. Who listens to them cry and whine and rage and laugh and prattle on about a million things that make no sense? She does.

- Who tries to be the best wife she can be? She does. Who supports her husband in his job, cares for the kids, and keeps the home running? She does. Who takes care of birthdays, including *his* family's birthdays? She does. Who handles Thanksgiving, Christmas, vacations, doctor visits, and school conferences? She does. Who shoulders a load of responsibility that would make a man cry out for his momma? She does.

Who has to bite her tongue when her husband whines about all the jobs he has to do around the home? She does. Who has to put up with his mother spoiling him and treating him like a baby? She does. Who agrees to have sex after a long day when she's finally looking forward to some rest? She does. At least, most of the time.

Who checks on her parents and his parents and looks after them? She does. Who works hard at her job outside the home? She does. After working all day, who comes home to a second shift of housework and child care? She does.

Who struggles with lack of energy, nervousness, sleeplessness, self-esteem, body image, and finding her unique, God-given purpose in the world? She does.

Does any of this sound familiar?

Who is tired, burned out, and stressed out of her head? She is. Why? Because she's doing too much. She's doing too much for everyone else. She's not taking care of herself. This is true of almost every woman I know—no matter how old she is or whether she's single or married.

If you're like Kate—and I'll bet you are—what will help you?

• Realize you're not Wonder Woman. You can't do it all. If you try to, you'll break down physically, emotionally, and spiritually. You'll lose yourself in the stressful whirlwind you have allowed to develop. You won't be the woman God wants you to be. You won't live the adventure He has for you.

- Learn to meet your needs in a balanced way. The healthiest women—and I think the godliest women— are those who get their needs met in a balanced way from four sources.

Before we take a look at these four sources that fill your need tank, a word to men: Even though this chapter is directed to women, you'll also get a lot out of it. It will help you understand and help your woman. Most of the stress-reducing principles apply to you, too.

Self

The first source for filling your tank is yourself. You meet a certain amount of your own needs. Nurturing yourself. Caring for yourself. Thinking realistically and positively about yourself. Developing a robust love for yourself. God wants you to love yourself in a healthy way. Jesus' words are, " 'You shall love your neighbor as yourself' " (Matthew 22:39).

It's your job to take care of yourself. In case you haven't noticed, no one else is going to do it. There are three actions I want you to take for yourself.

Personal Time

Get personal time out of the home on a regular basis (without the kids!). I call this the great escape. Actually it's the great escapes—plural—because you have to do it over and over. Most women, single or married, focus on the home and everything that needs to be done there. The trouble is that the jobs are never done. They keep coming! You've just done four loads of laundry when you notice a new pile of dirty clothes in the laundry basket. Arrh! You've just vacuumed the living room rug. You put the vacuum cleaner away and when you walk back into the room you see crushed crackers and cookie crumbs on the rug! No!

It's hard for you to relax when there are jobs to be done, right? Your husband doesn't notice or care if there are a thousand jobs undone. But you care. So to truly relax you've got to get out of there.

By personal time, I mean doing something that's fun for you. Grocery shopping doesn't count. Going to the discount retailer to buy things for the kids doesn't count. These are jobs! And they're done for somebody else! Your husband may think these count, but they don't. Do not use your personal time for jobs and errands.

Here are some examples of personal time:

- A fun shopping trip;

- Lunch or dinner with a friend;

- A Bible study;

- Going to a craft show;

- Going to the beach.

You can do it alone or with a friend or two. It's your time doing what you want to do. It's not for anyone else. It's for *you*. I recommend: 1) Once a week for two or three hours, perhaps using one weekday evening or part of Saturday; 2) Once a month for half a day or a full day; and 3) Once a year for an entire weekend. Schedule these times or they won't happen.

If you're married, make it clear to your husband that this is what you need. You'll have to go to him. He won't come to you and say, "Honey, I think you need regular personal time out of the home." Tell him this personal time will keep you from burning out and being a witch, it will give you more energy, and it will help you be a better sexual partner. That last one will get his attention.

Your husband may encourage you to get time away, but then he'll say, "But who's going to watch the kids?"

You'll say, "I don't know, honey! Who can watch our kids? It's either you or me, and since I'll be gone, I guess that leaves you!"

Your main obstacle to getting away will be *you*. You'll feel guilty. You'll feel selfish. You'll think, "There's no way I can leave! There are jobs to be done, the kids have needs, I don't want to get behind on my responsibilities."

I once met with a woman who was on the verge of major clinical depression. She was at her limit. She had small kids, worked outside the home, and had no time for herself. We worked out a deal: she was going to the beach for a weekend. Her husband was on board, not enthusiastically, but on board. Just before the planned weekend, she told me, "I'm not going to go."

My response to her was, "You've just chosen to go into a major depression, and it's your own fault."

Like so many women I've seen in therapy, this woman is functionally depressed. She's getting through life and handling all her many tasks, but she's exhausted and unhappy. Unless you want to be tired, burned out, and depressed, get out of the house on a regular basis. Do it with or without your husband's support. If he refuses to help with the kids, trade child care with friends or hire a babysitter. If you're a single mom, ask for help from your church. There are good people who will care for your children as a ministry.

God does not want you to crash and burn. He wants you to love yourself and nurture yourself so you can follow His plan for your life. His plan is not for you to be tired, burned out, and depressed. That's Satan's plan for you.

A Hobby

Every woman needs an interest, some activity that's fun. It gets you away from all the jobs you have to do. It reduces stress. It gives you energy and vitality. Perhaps most importantly, it nurtures your personhood. When you're doing your activity, you're not an employee. You're not a mom. You're not a wife. You're not a daughter. You're not a grandmother. You are *you*. You're doing something that you like to do, and it expresses who *you* are.

You may do your fun activity during your personal time. That's fine and a good time management strategy. It can be anything. Here are a few ideas to consider:

- scrapbooking;
- sewing;
- crafts;
- shopping;
- making stained glass or pottery;
- painting;
- taking a class;
- reading;
- playing a sport—golf, tennis, swimming;
- jogging or walking;

- going to the theater;

- going to the beach or a park.

Don't say to me, "I don't have the time." *Make* the time. Do your fun activity at least once every two or three weeks. More if possible. It will meet some important needs.

Regular Exercise
Consider these facts:

Fact: After eighteen years of age, we all go downhill physically unless we exercise regularly. It's also true that if, after age twenty-five, we continue to eat as we have been and do not follow a regular exercise program, we gain weight with virtually no limit. Therefore proper eating and weight control are also essential.

Fact: You have to exercise regularly if you want to stay physically, emotionally, and spiritually healthy.

Fact: Your body is the temple of the Holy Spirit (1 Corinthians 6:19–20), so it's important to take care of it.

These facts aren't earth-shattering news. You're not thinking: "Exercise? Wow! I've never heard this before!" You know it's important to exercise. You just have to do it. Forget your lame excuses. Get it done.

The experts recommend exercising for thirty minutes, three times a week. This is moderate exercise. You don't have to kill yourself. You're not training for the Olympics. You can walk, jog, or swim. There are all kinds of torture machines—I mean, exercise machines—you can use at home: stationary bike, treadmill, rowing machine, cross-country skiing machine, StairMaster. You might even have exercise machines already. Perhaps they're in museum-quality condition because you never use them!

A Best Friend

The second source for filling your tank is a best friend. There's something unique about a best friend. You can be totally open and honest with her, and she can be totally open and honest with you. You both get:

- feedback,

- support,

- accountability,

- laughter,

- shared experience,

- great conversation,

- spiritual connection,

- closeness.

This kind of best-friend closeness meets a lot of needs.

If you're engaged or married, you want to build a great marriage and be close to your man. I love marriage! I'm married, I do marital therapy, I do marriage seminars, and I've written books on marriage. But there are some needs that only a best friend can meet. I'm convinced that's by God's design.

Your man just doesn't get it. You're talking, sharing, pouring your heart out, and he just doesn't get it. At least, he doesn't get it all. Your best friend will get it. She'll understand you because she's a woman.

Your man can't listen to all your words. You have a lot, you know? He has limits. He tunes out. He goes into *the zone*. (I discussed this phenomenon in my book, *Men Are Clams, Women Are Crowbars*, Barbour, 1998.) You notice he's drifted off, so you ask him, "What are you thinking about?"

He replies, "Nothing." Your best friend will listen to you and all you have to say.

If you don't have a best friend, start praying that God will bring you two together. Start looking for her. She's probably in your neighborhood or in your church. She's out there.

Husband (or Fiancé or Serious Boyfriend)

The third source for filling your need tank is your husband (or fiancé or serious boyfriend). You don't have to have a man in your life. But if you do, then by God's design he's to meet certain emotional, physical, and spiritual needs. That doesn't mean he's going to meet your needs. He's *supposed* to do it. During courtship, he seems to meet your needs. After marriage, there can be a serious drop-off in need meeting.

There are three things I want you to understand about your man:

- Even a great husband can only meet 30 percent of your daily needs. That's it! Thirty percent. So don't look to him for any more than that.

- He doesn't have a clue about how to meet your needs. It's a safe bet that he's meeting a lot less than 30 percent of your needs. He tends to think of himself and has the intuition of a tree stump.

He'll pass by an overflowing laundry basket one hundred times without noticing. If he does notice, he'll say, "Hey, you need to do some laundry. I'm down to one pair of briefs."

You want to say, "No, you're down to one brain cell! Why don't *you* do a load of laundry?"

He'll watch television or be on the computer as you do job after job all around him: dishes, vacuuming, homework with the kids, dusting, laundry. Not once will he offer to help. It never dawns on him. He's in his own little world.

You say, "It sure would be nice to go out this weekend. You know, just the two of us." You say it right to his face.

He'll say, "Yeah, I guess it would." What's the matter with him? He's a man! Any kind of subtlety is lost on a man. Another woman, especially a friend, would instinctively know your needs. Not your man. No way. A man requires direct, clear communication, or he won't get the message.

- To get him to meet your needs, you must tell him exactly what your needs are:

  - Ask him to take you out on a date once a week. "Honey, I'd like to go on a date once a week. Let's choose Saturdays. This Saturday, I'll plan the date, next Saturday you'll plan the date, and so on."

  - Ask him to do certain chores. Discuss the exact chores you want him to do and reach an agreement. Write down the chores and post them. "Honey, I don't want to nag you."

- Ask him for a daily talk time. "Honey, I want to have half an hour to talk with you every day. Let's do it at 8:30 p.m., right after the kids go to bed."

- Ask him to pray with you. "Honey, I'd like us to pray together for five minutes, three times a week. Let's pray before our talk times on Monday, Wednesday, and Friday. Does that sound okay?"

- Ask him to approach you in a certain way for sex. Be gentle, but be specific. "Sweetheart, I can't respond well when you spring the idea of sex on me unpredictably. Please ask for sex in advance, the day before or at least the morning of, so I can be prepared. Even better, let's sit down each weekend and schedule our sexual times."

It's a good idea to actually sit down and write a letter to him describing in detail your needs. Then schedule a meeting and read it to him. Ask him to tell you and write you *his* needs. Have a series of meetings in which you nail down specific strategies to meet needs.

Being this direct and specific with your needs won't guarantee he'll meet them. But at least you have a chance. You probably think your man knows what your needs are. He doesn't. You probably think you communicate your needs clearly to your man. You don't.

God

Without question, God is the best source for meeting your needs. You have spiritual needs that only God can meet. There is a personal God that you can know intimately. He is the God of the Bible. He is the only God. He is the most wonderful, beautiful, powerful, and loving Person in the universe, and He wants to be close to you. He wants to meet your needs.

Know God
Come to know God through His Son, Jesus Christ. If you believe that Jesus Christ died on the cross for your sins and that He rose from the dead, you are a Christian (1 Corinthians 15:3–4). You know God.

Walk with God
Every day, spend time with Him. Talk to Him and listen to Him in prayer. As you struggle to heal from your emotional problem, be honest with God about your feelings and doubts and fears. Go ahead and vent with Him and question Him. That's what He wants you to do. That's how true faith is built.

Read the Bible
Read a portion of the Bible every day. Take a verse or two and, after reading it, meditate on it for a few minutes. Ask God to speak to you through His Word. Ask Him to give you the truths from His Word that you can use to replace your sinful, inaccurate thoughts.

Take God with You
Wherever you go, take God with you. Engage Him in an ongoing dialogue throughout your day. Tell Him your feelings. Tell Him your thoughts. Ask Him for truth, wisdom, guidance, and strength. No matter how weak your faith is, God loves you and wants to help you.

Tell God Your Worries
Take your worries to God. My friend Rick Reynolds says that

worry is a warning light on your dashboard prompting you to pray. Philippians 4:6–7 teaches that our interaction with God is the key to overcoming anxiety: "Be anxious for nothing, but in everything by prayer and supplication with thanksgiving let your requests be made known to God. And the peace of God, which surpasses all comprehension, will guard your hearts and your minds in Christ Jesus."

If your anxiety and worry are causing real problems, try this four-step fear-busting formula:

Step one. Let your anxiety (even panic) and all the irrational, inaccurate thoughts associated with it come into your mind. There's no way to stop them from coming in and your efforts to fight them increase your tension and anxiety levels.

Step two. Go to God in prayer and express to Him your worries, fears, and thoughts. Ask Him to help you identify your faulty thinking and find His truth.

Step three. Use a variation of the three-column technique discussed in chapter 9. Study the situation and your reaction to it and jot down information in these three columns:

- What are you worried about? (What has happened to trigger your worry and anxiety?)

- What are you thinking and feeling? (Your inaccurate, irrational, and distorted thoughts. Your lies. Also your feelings of anxiety, fear, and panic.)

- What's the truth? (With God's guidance, for which you have already prayed, write down the truth about the situation. Use scripture and the realistic, accurate insights God gives you about the event.)

Step four. Go again to God and tell Him all you have written in the three columns. Ask Him to help you dismiss your lies and believe His truths. Give your legitimate worries to Him and ask Him to deal with them. Ask Him for His peace.

You'll have to repeat step four several times because, after releasing your worries to God, you'll probably take them back. Several prayers may be necessary to give them back to God.

Do Your Work

1. Can you relate to Kate and all the jobs she is doing? Are you tired, burned out, and stressed to your limit? Can you admit you're not taking care of yourself?

2. If you answered yes to the questions above, share this with someone you love. Ask for this person's help in applying the stress-reducing strategies in this chapter.

3. What kind of regular personal time out of the home do you get? Do you have a hobby? Do you have a regular exercise program? Take action in these important areas.

4. Who is your best friend? If you don't have one, start praying and looking for her.

5. If you have a man in your life, ask him to read the section on spouses as a source for meeting needs and to comment on how clear you are in communicating your needs to him. Make a list of specific needs and work with him to negotiate how he will meet them. Follow the same process with his needs.

6. Do you know God personally through Jesus Christ? If not, are you ready to begin that relationship now? If you know God personally, how good are you at giving your worries to Him? If anxiety and worry are real issues for you, try my fear-busting formula for two weeks.

CHAPTER 14

TO BURY THE PAST, DIG IT UP: CONFRONT THOSE WHO HURT YOU

You have made great strides in your journey to emotional health. You have formed a support team. You have written an autobiography and answered the twelve questions. You have identified the payoffs and the high price of your problem. You have made progress in learning to think accurately and express your emotions in a healthy way. You have taken action to meet your needs and reduce your stress.

What you have to do now is heal from your unresolved past pain. You must face those who hurt you and release all the pain that they have caused. This step will be difficult, but it's essential.

Two Clients, Two Problems

Recently, I saw two clients in therapy. Each had a serious problem.

My female client had poor self-esteem. She didn't think she was attractive or smart. She had no confidence in her abilities. She had a chronic, low-grade depression. Her negative, distorted view of herself was crippling her career and her relationships with her family, friends, and God.

No one would have guessed that she saw herself this way. She had learned to be a good faker. In fact, she was attractive and smart and capable. But she didn't believe it. Why did she hate herself?

My male client couldn't express his emotions. He was a world-class stuffer. He didn't even feel his emotions. They were locked inside, way down deep. He was Mr. Logic, able to think rationally and solve problems. This style was effective at his job, but a disaster at home.

He came in to see me because his wife was on the verge of filing for divorce. She had spent fourteen years trying to get him to open up and share personally with her. All her efforts had failed, and she had hit the wall. She was weary and disgusted and ready to walk. Why couldn't this man express his emotions and share personal information with the woman he loved?

Unresolved Pain from the Past

As I worked with these two clients in therapy, a major source of their problems became clear quickly: unresolved pain from the past.

The woman with poor self-esteem had a poor relationship with her father. Growing up, he made no attempt to connect with her. He didn't give her attention, he didn't give her affection, and he didn't give her compliments. He was a decent guy. He was home a lot. He was a good provider. But she didn't get what she needed from him.

Every little girl needs to feel loved by her daddy, to feel special to him and close to him. When a dad doesn't do his job, self-esteem suffers. This woman didn't get her dad's love and approval, so she couldn't love herself.

The man with no emotional expression had a poor relationship with his mother. Actually it was worse than poor. It was abusive. He was the last child, and his mom had not wanted any more children. She alternated unpredictably from ignoring him to criticizing him. Ridicule, sarcasm, and fits of rage were the norm. She found ways to emasculate him every day of his life. His father was passive and did not protect him. His dad was a workaholic and rarely at home.

My client was on his own emotionally and had to find a way to cope. To protect himself and survive in his abusive home, he learned early on to deaden his emotions and stuff them deep inside. If he couldn't feel, he couldn't be hurt. That worked with his mother, but not his wife or his kids or God. He wasn't close to anyone.

The Past Is the Present

As with my two clients, your unresolved pain from the past will transfer to every part of your life now.

Your view of yourself is affected.

Your physical health is affected. Wherever your body is weak, that's where past pain will go.

Your emotional health is affected. Past pain helps produce depression, anxiety, severe stress, perfectionism, and anger. It can contribute to the development of sex, alcohol, gambling, drug, work, and food addictions.

Your career is affected.

Most seriously, your relationships are affected: spouse, children, extended family members, friends, and God.

You name the emotion and unresolved past pain will be a huge factor in its creation and maintenance. The past is not the past until you have faced it head-on and, with God's help, taken the necessary steps to heal from it.

My two clients did all the steps in my emotional health program that we've considered so far (and summarized in the first paragraph of this chapter), but they would not have healed completely without doing their work on their past pain.

If you have unresolved pain, it will remain inside you. It will fester and get worse. It will cripple you every day of every week of every month of every year for the rest of your life.

Do I have your attention? I hope and pray I do.

The Benefits of Your Work

When you have worked through your unresolved past pain, you'll be one step away from emotional health. There are six benefits of doing this work on your past:

1. You will completely correct—as much as anyone can this side of heaven—your problems in thinking and emotional expression. These problems began years ago when others hurt you. They became fused to the traumas in your past. I can't overstate the power and freedom that comes when you face the individuals who created your pain and taught you to be emotionally unhealthy. When you work through your past pain, you'll be able to think accurately and biblically and express your emotions in a healthy way.

2. You will be much healthier emotionally, physically, and spiritually. Because your emotional problem is under control and your emotional system is running smoothly, your health will improve dramatically in all areas. With your emotional problem out of the way, you can grow genuinely closer to God.

3. You will be able to truly and totally forgive all those who hurt you. Forgiveness is not a one-time choice. It's a tough, grueling, and painful process. When you face those who harmed you and speak the truth—what happened, your thoughts and feelings, and the impact on your life—then, and only then, can you forgive.

4. You will eliminate the transfer of past pain to your current close relationships. By no longer re-creating your past dysfunctional relationship patterns, you can build intimate relationships with your loved ones.

5. You will create closeness with those members of your support team who helped you work through your past pain. The experience of going to war with them will produce a unique and powerful bond.

6. You will give those who hurt you the opportunity to face the truth, repent, heal, and change. Their response is their business, but your responsibility is to speak the truth directly and seek reconciliation.

Biblical Support

The verses I quoted in chapters 10 through 12 provide the biblical support for facing and dealing with your past pain. You are to speak the truth to others, and there is no statute of limitations on the truth. The Bible also teaches you to confront your lies, express your emotions, express your anger, and speak directly to the people your thoughts and emotions are connected with.

Philippians 3:13–14 is often used to support the idea that the past ought to be left alone. I believe it teaches just the opposite: "Brethren, I do not regard myself as having laid hold of it yet; but one thing I do: forgetting what lies behind and reaching forward to what lies ahead, I press on toward the goal for the prize of the upward call of God in Christ Jesus."

Paul had a painful past, and he was determined to not be controlled by it. He honestly faced his past by talking about it and writing about it (Acts 26:9–11; 1 Corinthians 15:9; Philippians 3:5–8). He wanted to leave his past behind and move on to spiritual health and maturity in Christ.

You are being controlled by your painful past. It's time to leave it behind, so, as Paul was striving to do, you can move on to a new, healthy life in Christ. How do you forget what lies behind? By doing the work of facing those who hurt you and getting rid of the lies and emotional baggage these people instilled in you.

What Is Your Past Pain?
I gave only two examples of past pain with my two clients. I could give you many more. In fact, how many people are alive today on earth? That is how many examples I could give you. Everybody has pain from the past, including me. The only question is whether you have resolved it or not.

Let's talk about your pain. I'm going to ask you a series of questions. Give God, your spouse, and your accountability partner honest answers.

- What was your relationship with your dad like? Think about him now: the good, the bad, and maybe the ugly. Was he distant, unaffectionate, hard to get to know, stern, angry? Did he spend time with you? Did he compliment you? Did he criticize you? Did he ignore you? Did he say "I love you" often? Did he have a violent temper? Did he hit your mom, your siblings, or you? Did he yell at you? Did he call you names? Did he sexually abuse you?

- What was your relationship with your mom like? Answer the questions about your mom that you just answered about your dad.

- Was one or both of your parents alcoholic? Did they have any other addictions? What kind of marriage did your parents have? Did they express love to each other? Were they cold and distant? Did they have conflict and, if so, how did they handle it? Did they separate or divorce?

- If you had a stepmom or stepdad, how did this person treat you?

- Were you physically, emotionally, or sexually abused by someone inside or outside your family? Was the abuse done by a relative, a neighbor, a stranger, a boyfriend or girlfriend, a pastor, a coach, someone at church, or a teacher?

- Were you sexually promiscuous in the past? Did you have sex to feel loved, to get attention, or to get needs met?

- Have you been raped? Have you had an abortion? Have you gotten a woman pregnant and agreed to an abortion? Have you had a miscarriage? Have you given up a child for adoption?

- Have you not recovered from a divorce or the breakup of a significant opposite sex relationship? Were you abused or mistreated by a previous romantic partner? Has your spouse had an affair?

- Has someone you love died, and you're stuck in the grieving process?

- Have you done something in the past you're ashamed of? Something you've never told anyone? Something you've never worked through? Something you've been running away from?

- If I haven't mentioned your pain, what is it?

Whatever past pain you have, it's still there if you haven't faced it and healed from it. It's hurting you now and will keep on hurting you until you do something about it.

How do you stop your past from hurting you? How do you stop the transfer of past pain to your current life and relationships? How do you get healthy so you can move on to a better life? Here's how.

How to Forget What Lies Behind and Reach Forward to What Lies Ahead

To heal from your past unresolved pain, you need a strategy. A plan of attack. I have one for you. God has used it to heal many of my clients and I believe wholeheartedly that He wants to use it to heal you.

In chapters 15 through 17, I take my depressed client through the first three steps of my healing-from-past-pain program. In chapter 18 I cover the final step: the stages of recovery from loss. Here's a brief overview of these chapters:

Chapter 15

You must talk out your past pain in detail with several people you trust: a Christian therapist (if you have one), your spouse, your accountability partner, and possibly your pastor. If you have been harmed by more than one person, deal with them one at a time.

Then you will write what I call the *throw-up letter*. This is a raw, gut-level, visceral, and brutally honest letter to the person at the top of your past pain list. You'll go through the entire healing program with this person, and then repeat it with others if necessary. It's just as if you're emotionally throwing up on the paper. You get the details of the traumatic events out. You get out your pain connected to the details. You flush out your feelings. You identify the lies those individuals taught you. You describe the impact these individuals have had on your life.

There is no forgiveness in this letter. That comes later. This letter is a major step toward forgiveness.

Don't worry about grammar, punctuation, or sentence structure. Just let it rip. Let the words flow. Don't use a computer. Use pen and paper because this makes it more real and close to you and personal.

You will *not* send this throw-up letter. It's to be read to God and the key members of your support team. You may do several drafts of the letter, getting deeper and more detailed with each revision.

Chapter 16

You'll write a second letter to this first person who harmed you, the *truth-in-love letter*. With your raw emotions pumped out in the previous step, now you can focus on crafting a letter that expresses your emotions underneath anger and outrage: hurt, rejection, betrayal, sadness.

This letter is still honest and expressive, but not nearly as in-your-face intense. You cover the details, your pain, the lies, and the impact on your life in a more settled, matter-of-fact fashion. You tell the person the truths you could not or did not communicate back when the wounds were being inflicted. Writing now as an adult, you correct the lies you were taught with God's truths. You use release and forgiveness language. You may include some positives about the person, if there are any.

You'll mail this letter and ask for a response. Then you'll deal with the response. In follow-up letters, phone calls, or in-person contacts, you'll practice your new skills of expressing God's truths and your emotions. This dialogue will deepen and solidify your new, healthy way of living.

Chapter 17

When you have faced the pain others inflicted, you are ready to face the pain *you* have inflicted on others. One at a time, you'll deal with those individuals you have harmed in the past. First, you'll talk through what you did, your thoughts and emotions included, with the key members of your support team. Second, you'll write the *I'm-sorry letter*. It will include the details of what happened, your best explanation (not excuse) of why it happened, your request for forgiveness, and the clear willingness to engage in an ongoing dialogue with the person about the pain you caused.

Chapter 18

All traumatic past pain is experienced psychologically as a loss. In this final step, you'll learn how to navigate successfully through the four stages of recovery from loss.

These steps won't be easy. You can tell that by reading this outline of the road ahead. But, with God's help and your effort, they can make a huge difference in your life.

Let's go.

Do Your Work

1. What is your past unresolved pain? Who harmed you and contributed to the development of your emotional problem? Make a list of those who harmed you and what they did. Share the list with God and some trusted confidants.

2. Have you done something in the past you are ashamed of? Are you currently engaged in a sinful, destructive pattern or behavior? Tell this secret to your pastor, your spouse, and your accountability partner.

3. Have you harmed someone in the past? Who is it and what happened?

4. How is your past pain transferring to your current life and relationships? Is your emotional, physical, and spiritual health impacted? If so, how? In what close relationships do you see transfer?

5. As you prepare to face your past pain, pray with members of your support team for God's strength and courage to work through the steps of healing.

CHAPTER 15

VENT YOUR PAIN COMPLETELY: NO MORE EXCUSES, JUST THE TRUTH

As I listened to my depressed client talk about her dad in our first session, I immediately knew he was the original source of her depression. It was time to have her tell me about her dad in more detail:

> *My dad is a good man. He's always been a good man and a hard worker. Growing up, he spent long hours at work. I didn't spend much time with him. We didn't play together or have any personal conversations. I know he loved me, but I guess he couldn't show it. My mom has told me many times that he didn't know what to do with a girl. He pretty much let my mom raise me.*
>
> *Dad preferred to spend time with my brother. I think he was more comfortable doing guy things. He played sports with Mike, coached several of his teams, took him on hunting and fishing trips, and watched sporting events on television with him. Dad didn't have a clue that I wanted some special time with him, too. I did things with Mom, and Mike did things with Dad. That's just the way it was.*
>
> *Dad was often edgy and irritable. He was a Type A kind of guy. A real driver and a perfectionist. And critical. I can remember him criticizing my grades, the way I did my chores, some of the friends I chose, and certain hairstyles and clothes. I could never seem to please him, even though I tried and tried.*
>
> *He wasn't big on praise and compliments. He had high*

standards, and even when I did well and reached them, he said nothing. He just expected excellence and saw no reason to applaud it.

He only rarely said "I love you" to me. He wasn't a touchy-feely guy. He wasn't affectionate. I got a few hugs and pats on the head as a smaller child, but not many. And once I turned thirteen and began to develop physically, he never touched me again.

One thing about Dad really did bother me. When I was around twelve, I ran across a box of pornographic magazines in the attic. I was horrified! I knew they had to be my dad's, and I couldn't believe it. I wondered why he had to look at naked women. I felt dirty and ashamed.

I feel bad talking about my dad this way. He wasn't a perfect father, but what man is? He wasn't terrible. I think men of his generation had no idea how to raise a daughter. He's mellowed in recent years, and we have an okay relationship. It's funny, now that I think about it, how I still try to please him and get his attention and approval. That may never happen, but it's okay.

It's Got Dad Written All Over It

The original root and one of the continuing sources of her depression was her dad. The transfer of her pain from her father to her current life was obvious. Her dad was largely absent. He favored her brother. He was a critical perfectionist. He couldn't be pleased. He didn't praise or encourage her. He wasn't affectionate. He used women as sexual objects.

Her dysfunctional pattern of poor self-esteem, depression, lack of confidence, and superficial relationships began with her dad. It grew and developed because of her dad. Without meaning to, he shaped her into a person who hated herself and could not be open in her close relationships. How she perceived he felt and thought about her became how she felt and thought about herself.

Her autobiography helped her see the powerful influence of her dad. It also revealed the others on her unresolved-past-pain list: her mom, the boy who sexually molested her, and her college boyfriend. But it was her dad who started her depression rolling.

Excuses, Excuses, Excuses

At this point in her healing process, she'd done a lot of hard, excellent work. She had clearly improved. But it wasn't enough. I told her it was time to face the person who had done the most to create her unhappy, ineffective lifestyle: Dad. She didn't like me bringing up her dad. She didn't like it at all.

I shared with her how her dad had shaped and molded her into the depressed, passive, I'm-not-worthy person she had become. I showed her, in a specific point-by-point way, how her dad's treatment of her transferred to her life and relationships today. I said, "You're still acting like a little girl, trying to please your daddy."

After hearing my plan to work through the pain connected to her dad, she did not want any part of it. She didn't want to take the steps. She tried to talk me out of it. I expected and understood her fierce resistance. Dealing with a parent is a difficult and painful process to go through. But you don't get better until you do it.

Here are the reasons she gave to avoid her dad-work, and my responses:

Client: I love my dad!

Me: I didn't say you didn't love him. I'm sure you do. Love has nothing to do with it. You'll still love him after we're done. With your resentments out of the way, you'll love him more.

Client: I've forgiven him already. I prayed, and God gave me release.

Me: No, you haven't forgiven him. You don't forgive until you face the pain and clean it out with God's help. God doesn't use one-time prayers to heal. God will heal you and help you completely forgive, but He'll do it through the work.

Client: That was a long time ago.

Me: No, it's not. It's now. It's today. Your dad's behavior back then impacts you in significant ways in your current life. The work we'll do will finally put what happened years ago back into the past.

Client: I don't want to blame my dad for my problems.

Me: Don't worry, I won't let you blame him. Your depression and other problems are entirely your fault. I'm saying his mistakes played a huge role in creating who you are and how you see yourself and the world. You're still allowing him to control you. To break his power over you, you need to step up and deal with him honestly and directly.

Client: Dad was a good man.

Me: I'm not saying he wasn't a good man. I'm saying he was a lousy father and he hurt you deeply.

Client: He didn't mean to hurt me!

Me: You're right. He wasn't malicious. He didn't specifically plan to harm you. But hiding behind that truth won't get you better. If someone accidentally hits you in the head with a baseball bat, does it help to know he didn't mean to? It still hurts just as much, doesn't it? Your dad did hurt you, and we have to face that pain head-on.

Client: But he wanted the best for me!

Me: Let's say he did. So what? Intentions don't matter. What actually happened between you two is what matters.

Client: My dad had a bad childhood. That's why he mistreated me. It wasn't his fault.

Me: He's responsible for his actions. His bad childhood has nothing to do with your pain and your need to work it through. Pain is pain, and knowing the background of the one who inflicts it does not make it go away.

Client: My brother turned out all right. He seems pretty well-adjusted.

Me: Yeah, I guess you're the only rotten apple. The only crazy one. Come on! Your brother is living a decent life, but that doesn't mean he wasn't affected by his dad. I'm sure he has his own problems connected to his dad. Being the favorite child has its own burdens and problems. Anyway, I'm not talking to your brother. I'm talking to you.

Client: I don't feel anything, so there must not be any real pain there.

Me: Oh, you've got feelings all right. Very intense, painful feelings. They're just buried down deep. We'll dig them up.

Client: It could have been a lot worse.

Me: Yeah, I guess it could have been. But let's just address what did happen. It's bad enough. He hurt you and continues to impact your life.

Client: I don't think it's okay to be angry at my dad. I mean, that kind of anger isn't very Christlike. It's sin, isn't it?

Me: No, it's not sin. In fact, the anger I want you to express is healthy, normal, and Christlike. Stuffing it is part of the reason you're depressed. If you don't vent it, it will fester and lead to real sin: resentment, hostility, and bitterness. That's already happening to you.

Client: How can I honor my father the way the Bible commands if I do this work?

Me: The Bible also commands you to tell the truth. You will truly honor him by forgiving him and giving him a chance to change and reconcile with you.

Going Back in Time

After she got past her resistance, she was ready to talk about her dad and the hurtful things he did to her. As the process of verbalizing the pain caused by her dad began, we prayed that God would give her the two things she needed to heal: the specific memories and the emotional pain connected to those memories.

To help trigger the memories and the emotions that went with them, I had her use old photographs of her father. She went home for a weekend and looked through several family photo albums. Viewing these pictures of her dad and her family took her back in time and dredged up some intense emotions.

I also instructed her to call her brother and her mom and ask them to talk about her dad and what they remembered about his treatment of her. Her brother wouldn't open up. He refused to "dig up old stuff that's better left alone." Her mother, surprisingly, was honest and helpful. Her mom described a number of painful past events and said she was sorry her dad had not been a better father. My client asked her mom to not tell her dad about their conversation. She would be communicating with him when she was ready.

We talked through the pain of eight specific memories of her dad mistreating her. I had her describe to me in vivid detail—frame by frame—each of these life-shaping events. I told her God had given her these particular memories because they represented and covered all of her past pain with her father. When she relived these memories and expressed the emotions attached to them, she took a huge step forward in her recovery.

As she talked about these memories with me, she was able to get in touch with long-buried emotions: anger, rage, betrayal, sadness, shame, humiliation, guilt, and hurt. I gave her permission to vent freely, without holding back. She cried often, and I explained that crying was good for her. Tears are cleansing and healing.

I asked her to share these memories and her emotions with three other significant people: God, her husband, and her accountability partner. I told her all healing comes through relationship. The empathy, support, encouragement, and soul connection you get from certain special people is vital to becoming healthy.

The Throw-Up Letter

There's something about writing out emotional pain that's essential to genuine recovery. When you write to a specific person, you make the direct confrontation necessary for healing. When you write, you are forced to face your pain and express it in a personal, detailed way. Your words on the paper bring your traumatic life experiences from a shadowy, dark world into bright, clear reality.

It was time for her to write a throw-up letter to her dad. A ragged, intense torrent of truth and pain. A letter not to send, but to read to me and a few carefully selected people. I explained what the letter ought to contain and why she had to do it.

Before I sent her home to write the letter, we prayed that God through the Holy Spirit would guide her to put the right words on paper. We prayed for God the Father to give her the courage to be totally honest with her human dad and not hold back. We prayed that Jesus Himself would be right next to her and help her say all she needed to say and to feel all she needed to feel.

It took her three drafts to produce the detailed memories and deep emotions you'll read here. I have shortened this letter because her original was quite long and included all eight painful memories. This version will still give you a good idea of how this type of letter needs to be written.

Dad,

I've made excuses for you long enough. I'm through doing that. It's time for the truth. The truth is painful, really painful, and I've been scared of it for years. Scared of facing it. Scared of feeling it. I've lied to myself about you ever since I was a little girl. Stuffing my true feelings and pretending you were a good dad has cost me. It's a big part of my depression and relationship problems.

To break free of the power over my life that I've given you, I must be honest with you. Dad, the truth is, you blew it as my dad. You were not a good dad. You were a lousy dad, and you broke my heart over and over with your selfish, clueless, and critical behavior.

I will not let you off the hook because you were ignorant and didn't realize you were damaging me. You should have known! It doesn't take a genius to figure out your actions were cruel and insensitive and deeply hurtful to a little girl. Common sense should have told you that.

Mom stood by and said nothing as you systematically shredded my self-esteem and confidence. I'll be dealing with her later.

As I write these words, I can feel my stomach churning and bile coming up in my throat. My hand is literally shaking, but I'm going to keep on writing. My emotions are raw and intense. It's like they're all bubbling up to the surface after being submerged way down deep for years. About thirty years. I'm feeling rage. Burning anger. Disgust. Unbelievable frustration. Betrayal. Fear. Terrible sadness and hurt.

To clean out my pain and move toward forgiveness and my own healing, I've got to tell you the truth about certain memories. In detail. Well, here goes.

Dad, we spent so little quality time together. That was your fault. It seemed like you were always at the office. And when you were home, you weren't with me. You were reading the stupid paper or watching television or playing with Mike. I was right there! Why didn't you talk with me?

I'm fantasizing a scene right now in my mind. I'm in my little red jumper and pigtails, walking up to you and grabbing your paper and tearing it into small pieces. Then I'm screaming at you: "Here I am, Daddy! Play with me! Talk with me! Ask me how my day went! Give me the stinking time of day, Daddy!"

But you didn't give me your time. Day after day after day after day, you didn't. I wasn't important enough. I wasn't pretty enough. I wasn't smart enough. Did you know that's what I thought? No, you didn't know that because you just didn't get it!

I remember the time you promised me you'd play tea party with me the next day. I had just gotten the princess tea set for my birthday, and I invited you to my first tea party. How stupid was that? Like you were going to come! I guess I was still naive enough to think you'd care enough to show up for at least one crummy little tea party.

I fussed over that tea set most of the next day, getting it just right for my daddy. I must have spent hours watching for you at the window to get home from work. I just knew you'd come. But you didn't. Another late night at your all-important job. I went to bed, and you still weren't home. I cried and cried in my bed.

You came in late that night and came to my room, probably because Mom told you that I'd waited for you all day. You said, "Sorry, honey." You know what, Dad? "Sorry, honey" doesn't cut it! Why didn't you show up on time? Why didn't you reschedule the tea party? Why didn't my tears that night cause you to change and spend time with me? I'll tell you why. Because your job was more important to you than I was. As least, that's how I felt.

You broke my five-year-old heart that day. I'm crying now as I write these words. What you did was cruel. Mean. And you hurt me way down deep. It makes me furious and sad at the same time that you missed me. You missed this chance to connect with me, and you missed a million other chances.

You and I both know that one of the big reasons why you ignored me was my brother, Mike. You preferred him over me. You spent most of the little free time you had with him. I don't blame Mike. I blame you.

I know many fathers tend to favor sons. I don't care! Do you hear me? I don't care! For years and years, I watched you play with Mike. Did you ever notice the little girl watching at the window as you threw the ball in the front yard with Mike? Did you ever notice the little girl watching at the window as you and Mike went off to baseball, football, or soccer practices? Did you ever notice the little girl watching at the window as you and Mike drove off on a fishing or hunting trip? That little girl was me. And I was crying. Devastated. I died a little more every time you chose him over me.

Was there something wrong with me? Yes, there must have been. That was the conclusion I came to, Dad. Because I was invisible to my daddy, I must be pretty worthless. I can remember wishing I were a boy because boys were obviously special. Do you see what you did to me? You big, dumb ox, why didn't it occur to you to take me on those hunting and fishing trips? Girls can do those activities, too.

It was about just being with you, my daddy.

I think I began to hate myself somewhere in here. Always coming in second to Mike made me feel like a worthless, useless piece of garbage. It would have been better if you'd ignored Mike, too. Then at least it would have been fair, and I wouldn't have concluded that there was something wrong and bad about me.

Dad, you were so critical of me as I grew up. I was already hating myself because you ignored me, but you had to add to my misery and self-loathing by criticizing everything about me. Didn't you know that you needed a loving relationship with a child before you had the right to criticize her? Didn't you know that praise and encouragement should far outweigh any criticism of a child? No, of course you didn't know those things. And I paid dearly for your ignorance.

About the only words I heard from you were negative. I couldn't seem to do anything right. I couldn't please you. My chores weren't good enough. My grades weren't good enough. My hair wasn't good enough. My clothes weren't good enough. My friends weren't good enough.

I wasn't good enough. You made me believe that, Dad. I've carried that message around in my head for years. This letter is going to help me get it out of my head. I am good enough! I was always good enough! You couldn't see it! You couldn't see all the good things about me!

I remember handing you one report card. I think I was in fifth grade. It had all As and only one B in math. You didn't even mention the As. All you said was: "You'll have to work harder to get that math grade up to an A." Thanks for driving a stake through my heart. If you'd known me better, you would have known I was never good at math. I worked hard for that B, and it was a great grade for me!

Remember that morning I was on my way to school and you ridiculed my appearance? I'll bet you don't. I was in seventh grade, awkward and extremely self-conscious. You lowered the newspaper—for once—and glanced up at me. You said my hair was a mess and my clothes were too tight. You told me to change unless I wanted to look like a prostitute. How dare you! You embarrassed and humiliated me!

I fled back to my room and sobbed uncontrollably. Did you come back and apologize? No. Good old Mom tried to comfort me by saying, "That's just your father. He didn't really mean it." A lot of help that was. I hate you for that cruel criticism of me. That day you convinced me I was ugly. I still feel that way, but I'm determined to change my mind. I don't believe I'm beautiful yet, but I'm working to get there.

Dad, your lack of affection was the final nail in the coffin of my self-esteem. I already hated myself and thought I was stupid and unworthy because of your lack of attention and criticism. When you stopped touching me in middle school, I assumed I was ugly and completely undesirable to the opposite sex.

I'm angry now about all these behaviors of yours, but I think it was too scary to be angry at you back then. I just stuffed my anger and hurt and turned it on myself. It was safer to be angry at myself and hate myself.

I will never, ever, forget that day when I found your porn stash in the attic. I was shocked and horrified and filled with a feeling of anguish. It was so disgusting to think that my dad was looking at these naked women! Right then I knew why you didn't think I was pretty. You preferred women who were thin and huge-chested and glamorous and. . .perfect physically. I couldn't match that ideal.

Dad, that's all I have to write. I'm drained and

exhausted. I don't have enough paper to write all the bad,
hurtful things you said and did to me. I'm praying that God
will somehow use these specific memories to cover all the pain
you caused me.

I've written the truth, the way I remember living it.
Digging all this up has really hurt, but I hope and pray
my honest expression of emotions will with God's help stop
forever your negative impact on my life. This is, I pray
fervently, a big step toward forgiving you and moving on.

I had her read this letter to an empty chair in my therapy office. I asked her to imagine her dad was sitting in the chair and that she was reading her letter directly to him. Before the reading, we prayed that God would use the letter to help her release her pain, heal from what her dad did to her, and forgive him.

Just before reading it, she hesitated and told me she thought the letter was too harsh.

I asked, "Is it the truth?"

She replied, "Yes, it is."

So I answered, "That's all that matters. You can only heal and forgive when you express the truth about events and the emotional pain connected to them."

She read the letter, and it was an intense experience. A lot of tears. A lot of anger. A lot of hurt. A lot of emotions. God helped her clean out a great deal of trauma and pain that day. We prayed again for His healing touch through this work. It was a breakthrough for her in her healing journey. She told me she felt like a huge load had been lifted from her shoulders.

Following my instructions, she read the letter to three important support team members: God, her husband, and her accountability partner, in that order. These additional readings deepened and accelerated her recovery because a shared experience is a healing experience.

Finally, I had her and her husband burn the throw-up letter. The smoke and ashes symbolized the death, the end of all that past pain with her dad and its control over her.

But even though this letter had purged her system of a huge amount of emotional garbage, she still had more work to do. She was not completely healed from her dad's impact on her life. She had not completely forgiven him.

I told her she was ready to take the next step in her recovery from her dad-work. I warned her that what I was about to ask her to do would be extremely scary. It would be extremely difficult. It would be a lot harder than the throw-up letter. She would need God's presence and power to carry it off, but it would be worth the effort. True healing and forgiveness would be hers.

It was time for her to deal directly with her dad.

Do Your Work

1. Pray on your own that God will help you face the truth about those who have hurt you in the past. Pray this same prayer with someone you love and trust.

2. Do you recognize any of the classic excuses to avoid facing the pain that a parent or another person caused? Which excuses have you used?

3. Talk openly and honestly about your past pain and those who caused it with God in prayer, and with a support team member.

4. Write a throw-up letter to the person on your list who caused you the most pain. Don't hold back. Let your emotions go. Make it as long as you need to. Before you write, pray—and have your support team pray—that God will give you the memories and the pain.

5. Read your throw-up letter to three people: God and two members of your support team. Pray individually and with your support team members that God will use this letter to bring about healing and forgiveness.

CHAPTER 16

I'VE GOT SOME THINGS TO TELL YOU: DEAL DIRECTLY WITH THE PEOPLE WHO HAVE HARMED YOU

I asked my client if she wanted to truly and completely forgive her father for all the pain he had caused her. Of course, she said, "Yes."

I asked her if she was absolutely sure of her answer.

She gave me a funny look and replied cautiously, "Yes, I'm sure. Why did you ask me twice? I have a funny feeling I'm going to have to do some more hard work with my dad in order to forgive him."

"You're right about more hard work," I told her. "The bad news is, the two actions I want you to take with your dad will be difficult. The good news is, when you've done them you will have totally forgiven your dad. The first action is to write him a truth-in-love letter and mail it to him. The second action is to deal with his response to that letter. Let me explain both of these."

The *Truth-in-Love Letter*

I continued, "The truth-in-love letter brings about healing, change, and forgiveness. It will help *heal* you from the pain your dad inflicted on you. It will lead to *change*. You'll be a new person who will think and express emotions in healthy ways. Finally, you will forgive your dad. You'll release him from the debt he owes you. You'll no longer harbor resentment, bitterness, and hurt for what he did to you. Your pain will be flushed out, and it will no longer have any power over you.

Your dad's powerful emotional hold on you will be broken, and you can move on with your new life.

"Your truth-in-love letter, although based on your throw-up letter, has a different tone and approach. It will be shorter and more to the point. Because you have already expressed your painful emotions, this time your intensity will be lower. It will be a letter in which you correct the emotional damage he did to you. It's a letter of truth and forgiveness expressed in a loving, Christlike manner.

"I want you to take each trauma you covered in your throw-up letter and do three things.

"Tell the story. Briefly describe what happened, the pain you felt, the impact on you, and how it distorted your thinking and emotions.

"Tell the truth. Give him the truth in the trauma. Tell him he was wrong to treat you this way and why he was wrong. Tell him the truth, God's truth, about you.

"Tell him what you'd do and say now. For each traumatic event, tell him how you'd handle it now as a healthy, truth-telling adult.

"When you're finished writing this letter, read it to your husband and accountability partner. Pray with them that God will use it to bring about healing, change, and forgiveness for you and your dad. Then mail it. Keep a copy so you can be better prepared to deal with his response. Ask him to respond first with his own letter. Then you and he can have a dialogue, if he's open to it, by e-mail, phone, or in person."

Dealing with the Response

"Your job is to face your dad—via letters, e-mails, phone calls, or in person—and discuss his reaction to your truth. You will stand firm on what you have written, while listening to his point of view. You'll restate your truth, defend it if necessary, and answer his questions and challenges.

"What you're doing is practicing the new you: honest, assertive, speaking the truth in love, and expressing your emotions in healthy ways. It's what psychologists call a corrective emotional experience. That's a fancy way of saying, 'You go, girl!' This process of responding to him will solidify and lock in your changes. If you can do this kind of straight talking with your dad—and you can—you can and will do it with anyone."

Do I Have to Deal Directly?

As you can imagine, my client wasn't wild about these two actions. I expected her resistance. Just about every client I've worked with has tried to avoid writing the truth-in-love letter and dealing with the response.

She asked me, "Haven't I done enough already? Can't I just tell my dad-pain to you and my support team, read the throw-up letter, and take it to God and leave it all with Him?"

I told her, "That's not enough. It's a good start and these steps have partially healed you, but it's not enough. The Bible is clear that we must forgive others. Read Matthew 18:21–35 and Luke 17:3–4. We must forgive others no matter how serious the offense. No matter how many times we're harmed. No matter what attitude the other person displays to us. If we don't forgive others, God won't forgive us.

"The Bible is also clear about *how* we are to forgive. The Bible says deal directly. Remember Matthew 5:23–24, Matthew 18:15–17, and other passages teach us to face those with whom we have issues of conflict, sin, and pain. God is talking to you through these passages.

"It's through the process and hard work of forgiveness that

you heal and change. This is why God wants you to deal directly with others. Yes, take all your pain to God. But in addition, He wants you to take it to the source, to the person who created the pain for you. When you do that, you've obeyed God and will be a changed person. God also wants you to deal directly because it gives the other person and the relationship an opportunity to heal. This isn't just about you. It's about the other person, as well."

She wasn't quite done yet with her resistance. She said, "I've heard several well-known authors and radio pastors teach that forgiveness is a choice. They say that all you have to do is pray about it and choose to forgive."

I said, "If only it were that easy! That way avoids all the hard work, doesn't it? When does God ever allow us to take the easy road to character and spiritual maturity? Forgiveness is not just a choice! It's a series of difficult and painful steps which require time, effort, and faith in God."

She made one more attempt. "I've heard a number of experts, all Christians, recommend writing a letter to the person who harmed you in which you ask his or her forgiveness for all your mistakes in the relationship. Sometimes they say send it, and sometimes they say tear it up and don't send it."

I responded, "Yes, I'm familiar with this approach and the experts who espouse it. They're well meaning, but they're wrong. How does this approach lead to you forgiving the person? If you are guilty of mistakes, then it makes sense for you to directly admit those mistakes and ask for forgiveness. But what about the other person's mistakes?

"This strategy of asking for the other person's forgiveness is biblically incorrect. The Bible says speak the truth and deal directly. Just mentioning your mistakes—if there are any—isn't the whole truth. And not sending the letter is in violation of the Bible's teaching to deal directly.

"Psychologically, their approach is also incorrect. If something is biblically incorrect, it's also psychologically incorrect. These experts are not full-time clinical psychologists, so they don't understand how forgiveness really is accomplished. I am and I do. I can't tell you how many clients I've seen who tried it their way and were not able to forgive.

"Here is the biblical and psychological truth: You forgive when, and only when, you express your pain directly with the one who harmed you. That's what God says in the Bible, and I'm going to go with God's plan.

"Here are the only exceptions to dealing directly: if you have no idea where the person is, like that pervert who sexually molested you as a child; if the person is dangerous and very likely to cause you physical or emotional harm; if the person has some form of dementia or other brain disease that severely limits intellectual capacity; if the person is fragile because of a serious, life-threatening illness; or if God truly reveals to you that you are not to deal directly."

In these situations, God will help you completely heal and forgive without any direct contact with the person who harmed you. Venting your pain with a trusted confidant and writing the letters will be enough. In some cases, I've had clients visualize the person who harmed them in an empty chair. Then, they express their pain verbally and read letters to the person—just as if the person was in the chair.

A Sample *Truth-in-Love Letter*

I prayed with my client and asked God to guide her in the writing of this second letter. She also prayed with her support team members as she prepared to write. Here is her letter in its entirety:

Dear Daddy,

I've got some things I have to tell you. The truth is painful, really painful, and I've been scared of it for years. I have done a lot of work on what happened between you and me in my childhood. Even though it wasn't your intent, some of the things you said and did hurt me deeply and were a big part of creating my depression. I've been angry at you for years, and it's time to let that go and forgive you.

My purpose in this letter is to tell you the truth and share my emotions about how you harmed me as a child. By doing this, I will forgive you and take a big step toward my healing as a person. I also want my words to lead to a healed relationship between you and me. With the truth expressed, that can happen.

I want to be clear, Dad, that I'm not blaming you for my depression and other personal and relational problems. I'm an adult, and I own those problems. I've made plenty of bad choices that have produced and maintained my depression. To be free of depression and live in a healthy way, I need to deal directly with all those who played a role in my depression's development. You are one of those, along with a few others.

I know what I write is going to hurt you a lot. That's not why I'm writing this, but I know it will happen. It is the truth—my truth—and I ask that you read it with an open mind. Take a few days to pray about it and process it, then please write me back.

To clean out my pain, forgive you, heal, and hopefully heal our relationship, I've got to tell you the truth about certain memories. Well, here goes.

Dad, you spent so little quality time with me. You were at the office, reading the paper, watching television, or playing with Mike. I really wanted to spend time with you, but you didn't seem interested. I felt angry, hurt, and rejected. And those feelings went on inside me for a long time, because you didn't spend time with me all during my childhood.

I remember the time you promised me you'd play tea party with me the next day. I had just gotten the princess tea set for my birthday, and I invited you to my first tea party. You came home late from work, and there was no tea party. You came in to my room, late, and said, "Sorry, honey." Dad, that hurt me badly. I felt abandoned and rejected. I believed I wasn't pretty enough or smart enough or interesting enough for you. These are incorrect thoughts I've believed for years. The truth is that I am pretty and smart and interesting.

Dad, here's what I'd say to you about that tea party now, as an adult: "I'm angry, I'm hurt, and I feel rejected that you missed our tea party. I accept your apology, but I need you to spend time with me. I am a neat, interesting person whether you spend time with me or not. I will not let your lack of interest in me determine how I feel and think about myself."

Your relationship with Mike was a source of great pain for me. I understand now many fathers tend to favor sons, but I didn't understand it back then. I needed your attention to feel special, and I didn't get it. I was so hurt—devastated, really. Always coming in second to Mike contributed to my growing hatred of myself. I felt worthless. Of course, I couldn't express these emotions to anyone, so I just did a lot of crying in my room.

Dad, I want you to know that I am a worthy person even though you didn't spend much time with me. Your absence did hurt me and negatively shape my thinking, but I've moved beyond that now. As an adult, I say to you, "Dad, I'm angry and deeply hurt that you spend all your free time with Mike. I'm just as worthwhile and special as him,

*and I'm fun to be with. Your time with me has nothing to do
with my value as a person."*

*Your regular criticism of me also played a part in the
development of my poor self-esteem and depression. Mom
has told me that you grew up in a critical home, but I wish
you wouldn't have been so hard on me. I was a sensitive
girl—most girls are—and your critical comments about my
chores and grades and hair and clothes and friends damaged
my confidence in myself.*

*One incident stands out to me. One time I was on my
way to school, and you said my hair was a mess, my clothes
were too tight, and I had to change unless I wanted to look
like a prostitute. Dad, I was embarrassed and humiliated!
I cried and cried in my room, but you never said "I'm sorry."
That was no way to talk to your daughter. That incident,
and others like it, convinced me I was ugly and low-class.*

*As an adult, I would have said: "Dad, how dare you
call me a prostitute! I'm angry and insulted. I also don't
appreciate your critical tone. My choice of clothes may not
please you, but that doesn't make me a loose, promiscuous girl.
When you're ready, I'd like an apology. I am an attractive,
classy female, and nothing you can say will change my mind."*

*Dad, I have to mention your box of pornographic
magazines and videos in the attic. I found that box when I
was almost out of elementary school. That shocked me, Dad,
and made me angry at you for Mom's sake. I lost trust in you
and have struggled to trust men ever since. Most of all, this
discovery intensified my belief that I wasn't pretty. If my dad
considered these "perfect" women to be attractive, then I must
not be pretty at all.*

*As an adult, I would have come to you and said,
"Dad, I just found your box of pornography. I'm angry and*

disgusted and disappointed. I'd like you to get rid of
that stuff and get some professional help for your problem.
Your pornography problem does not mean I can't trust other
men or that I'm not attractive. I can trust my husband,
and I am pretty. My husband thinks I'm beautiful and so
does God."

Well, that's it. This was difficult to write, and I'm sure
difficult for you to read. It was necessary in order for me to
obey the Bible, which teaches us to "speak the truth in love"
(Ephesians 4:15) and to speak directly to the person you
have issues with (Matthew 5:23–24, 18:15–17).

Dad, I know and appreciate your good, positive traits:
You've stayed with Mom in a stable marriage, you worked
hard to provide for our family, you paid for my college
education, you've been generous to my husband and me
financially, you've got a good sense of humor, etc. But I had
to speak the truth about the negative things because it was
those events that shaped my thinking and emotions.

I'm sorry for taking so long to tell you the truth. I've
resented you for too long and said nothing. That hurt me and
you. I was wrong to harbor resentment, and I ask for your
forgiveness. My resentment is gone now. I forgive you for all
you did to hurt me.

I no longer need your approval. I'd like it, but it's not
necessary. I have God, my husband, my kids, and a few good
friends to meet my needs. Dad, this letter is the truth. My
truth. I ask you to believe it. I also ask you to think and
process for a few days, and then write me a response. I'd like
to know what you think and feel about what I've written.
Why do you think you treated me in these ways? After I
receive your letter (if you write one), let's have a dialogue
about all this—by phone or in person. I think it will only be

*a few talks to clear the air and hopefully get our relationship
on track.*

*Dad, I love you and want to be closer to you. I believe we
can work through this past pain together and start over as a
father and daughter.*

The Response

My client read this letter to me and her support team members.
Then she mailed it. She waited on pins and needles to see how
her dad would respond. Surprisingly he mailed back a letter one
week later in which he apologized for his behavior, asked for her
forgiveness, and shared some things from his past that may have
contributed to his poor fathering. They had a few phone calls
and one in-person conversation about these painful issues and
were able to heal their relationship.

I refer to his response as surprising because, sadly, it is not
the usual response. Most parents—indeed, most individuals on
your past-pain list—will have a negative response to your truth-
in-love letter. Here are some of the most common responses my
clients have gotten:

- Complete denial. "What you say happened never
  happened. You're a liar." Or you're crazy and made
  all this up. Or your shrink has fooled you and
  manipulated you into thinking all this happened.

- Complete rebuttal. A form of denial in which all your
  points are refuted. A different version of each event is
  offered. Usually accompanied by personal attacks on
  you. Your mistakes and sins are brought up and made
  the only issues. "It's all your fault."

- "I'm sorry you're so troubled by the past." Not "I'm

sorry for how I hurt you." A variation of the previous response.

- It wasn't as bad as you say it was. "Yes, some of the things you brought up did happen, but you overstated your case. You overreacted, and your feelings are too intense. These things occur in life, and you shouldn't make a big deal out of them."

- This is all in the past; let it go. This response is an admission that these events did occur, but it's also an absolute unwillingness to acknowledge or discuss them because they happened in the past. "It's all over with now, and we can't and shouldn't go back and deal with it." Sometimes you'll get a blanket general apology with this response and sometimes you won't. Often this approach includes a plea to start over now with a new relationship.

- "If I offended or hurt you, I'm sorry." The word *if* calls into question what you're saying and is a lame way of trying to avoid any responsibility.

- The spiritual approach. "I'm close to God now, and everything that happened is under the blood of Jesus." The person is hiding behind Jesus' sacrifice on the cross to escape dealing with the truth.

- You're not much of a Christian. "If you were a real, faithful Christian, you would not have to bring up these past events. If you really loved God, you'd just forgive me. I thought Christians were supposed to be loving and forgiving."

- "How could you bring up all these painful memories?

I'm hurt and devastated. Poor me." The spotlight shifts to his or her pain, not your pain. Usually combined with all the good things this person did for you.

- Circle the family wagon. Family members are quickly contacted and signed up as supporters. The strategy is to discredit you and isolate you.

- No response at all. Total silence. Your letter is not acknowledged. You are ignored. It's a refusal to address any of the issues you raised.

- Complete rejection. A harsh, brutal assault that is often accompanied by severing the relationship. "You're out of the will, disowned, and cut off until you humbly apologize for your horrible letter and beg for forgiveness."

No matter the response you get, your job is to stand on the truth that you have communicated. You do not waver from your biblical responsibility to directly speak the truth in love. You make it clear that, when the recipient is ready, you want to engage in an honest and reasonable dialogue about the truth of the past.

The good news is that the other person's reaction has no bearing on your healing. Because you told the truth, you will heal regardless of the response. An honest, positive response is, of course, necessary for reconciliation and an improved relationship. But you only have control over what *you* do and say.

If you have ongoing contact with this person who harmed you, you must continue to speak the truth in love. If the person hurts or offends you in the present, you need to tell him or her every time. This ongoing assertive expression of the truth will keep your emotional system cleaned out and allow you to continue to forgive.

I recommend you follow this same approach to unresolved past pain with every person who significantly harmed you in the past. Take them one at a time. In my depressed client's case, after working the process with her dad, she worked through the steps with her mom, the pervert who sexually abused her, her college boyfriend, and God.

Do Your Work

1. What are your reservations about writing a truth-in-love letter? What do you fear the most?

2. Have you bought into some of the popular Christian teaching on forgiveness? What popular approaches have you heard and which ones do you believe? Compare these how-to-forgive approaches with what the Bible says. Read the verses mentioned in this chapter, talk with your support team members about forgiveness, and pray that God will direct you in this critical area.

3. Pray alone and with one or more of your support team members for God's help in writing the truth-in-love letter. Write it, read it to key support team members, and mail it.

4. What kind of response do you think you'll get from this person? Practice your assertive, biblical reaction to the possible responses.

5. Follow these steps—make up a past-pain list, pray for God's help to face and express the truth, identify your excuses, talk your pain out with your support team, write the throw-up letter, read the throw-up letter to your support team, write the truth-in-love letter and send it, and deal with the person's response—with each of the people who have significantly harmed you. Do them one at a time.

CHAPTER 17

MAKE AMENDS WITH THOSE YOU HAVE HURT: ADMIT YOUR MISTAKES AND ASK FOR FORGIVENESS

You've worked through your unresolved past pain. You've talked it out, written the letters, and dealt with the responses of those who hurt you. Now you need to turn your attention to those *you* have significantly hurt in the past.

Reasons for Making Amends

Making amends is important for four reasons:

It's God's Command

You don't need a seminary degree to understand Matthew 5:23–24. Jesus says, " 'Therefore if you are presenting your offering at the altar, and there remember that your brother has something against you, leave your offering there before the altar and go; first be reconciled to your brother, and then come and present your offering.' "

There are others who have something against you. You have intentionally or unintentionally harmed them. Jesus says you must go to them and attempt to make it right.

It's Part of Your Healing

You must clean out *all* the pain in your past relationships for complete healing to occur. Any leftover pain will remain, fester, and continue to damage you. And Satan will take advantage of it (2 Corinthians 2:11).

It Gets Rid of Your Guilt

Guilt is one of the most draining and destructive emotions. It weakens you emotionally, physically, and spiritually. It acts as a cancer, eating away at your insides. As the days, weeks, months, and years go by, it does more and more damage. Satan is the accuser of Christians (Revelation 12:10), and he loves to keep you chained to your guilt.

In addition to Satan's efforts to feed your guilt, there are a number of other possible reasons your guilt stays stuck to you:

- You minimize it and convince yourself what you did wasn't that bad.

- You rationalize it and try to believe what you did was okay.

- You blame someone else for what happened.

- You play God and decide to punish yourself forever for what you did.

On a deeper level, you may still carry guilt because you haven't worked through the pain you caused, so that pain remains inside. That leftover pain has to go somewhere, and guilt is one of those places.

Scripture is crystal clear with the wonderful message that God forgives you for every sin you have committed and ever will commit. The only exception is the sin of not believing that Jesus Christ died for your sins and rose again. My pastor, Paul Phair, made these points about God's forgiveness in a sermon:

- God forgives instantly (1 John 1:9);

- God forgives completely (Colossians 2:13–14);

- God forgives repeatedly (Matthew 18:21–22);

- God forgives and forgets (Isaiah 43:25; Jeremiah 31:34).

All you have to do is ask God for forgiveness (1 John 1:9), and He gives it to you. But *knowing* you are forgiven and *feeling* forgiven are two different things. The steps in this chapter will create the feeling of forgiveness that you so desperately want and need.

It's Good for the Person You Harmed
As Matthew 5:23–24 teaches, God desires reconciliation and restoration in relationships. Dealing with those you have harmed will help them heal, also. They have been carrying around the pain you've caused. Facing them and asking for forgiveness gives them a chance to heal and gives you an opportunity to mend the relationship. Their healing and a reconciled relationship may not happen, but God says it's your responsibility to give them that chance.

Healing from Your Mistakes
Follow these five steps in dealing with a person you have harmed:

Pray for God's Forgiveness
Confess your sin privately to God and claim His forgiveness (1 John 1:9). Pray this same prayer with someone you love and trust (Matthew 18:19–20).

Talk through Your Sin with a Team Member
The Bible instructs us to bear one another's burdens (Galatians 6:2). Find a person you trust with your life and put the burden of your sin on that support team member. You always heal in relationship. Always.

The story of King David's adultery, his murder of Uriah, and his confession is told in detail (2 Samuel 11–12; Psalm 51). Why? Because the details are important to the recovery process. Tell your burden bearer every detail of the story of how you harmed the other person. Your support team member's empathy and encouragement will aid in your healing and give you the courage to take the next step.

Write the I'm-Sorry Letter

When you create your I'm-sorry letter, you write out, in specific detail, what you did to cause pain and harm to this person. It's a full, complete confession of your sin. This specific confession is good for you because it cleans out your emotions, including guilt. It's good for the other person because it builds understanding. The person you're writing to will see that you grasp the meaning and impact of what you did.

You apologize several times and ask for forgiveness. You acknowledge that it will almost certainly take him or her time to forgive you.

You invite a response to your letter in any way the person chooses: a letter, an e-mail, a phone call, or a personal visit. You offer to dialogue with the person if that is needed for healing. You'll listen to venting and answer all questions. You indicate you will do whatever it takes to foster forgiveness and reconciliation.

When you have completed the letter, read it to God and key support team members. Pray with your supporters that God will use the letter to heal you, the other person, and the relationship.

Mail the Letter

If you can locate the person, mail the letter. Provide all your contact information. The exceptions to mailing the letter are the same as for the truth-in-love letter. Don't mail the letter if the person is dangerous and likely to cause you physical or emotional harm, if the person has some form of dementia or other brain disease that severely limits intellectual capacity, if the person is fragile because of a serious, life-threatening illness, or if God truly reveals to you that you are not to deal directly with the person.

This is not a business letter, so don't use a computer. A handwritten letter is much more personal.

Engage in Dialogue

If the person wants to communicate with you about your actions, do it. Remember, all you are responsible to do is go and tell the truth and seek to be reconciled. You work on your half of the bridge of reconciliation; the other person is responsible for the other half. The person could ignore your confession, respond by saying that what you did was no big deal and you didn't have to confess, or blast you with red-hot rage and refuse to forgive. Whatever the response, you'll still be forgiven by God and get rid of your guilt.

Follow the above five steps with each of the people you have harmed.

Two Sample Letters

My depressed client identified five people she felt she had significantly harmed: a high school acquaintance about whom she had spread vicious rumors, her husband, her children, her aborted baby, and God. Below are two of her I'm-sorry letters.

> Dear Bonnie,
>   Yes, I have given you a name. Even though you never

took a breath, you deserve a name. You are my precious Bonnie, the baby I killed so many years ago. I've spent years and years trying to avoid you and fool myself into believing what I did was okay. That I had no choice. That it was my boyfriend's fault. That I am forgiven.

I am forgiven by my gracious God, but I have never felt forgiven. I have never felt any of the burden of my guilt lifted. I believe by facing you and writing out my confession, I can feel God's forgiveness and find a way to move on.

Bonnie, I had sex with my boyfriend and that is how you came into being within me. The sex was a mistake, but you were not. When I found out I was pregnant, I was absolutely terrified. I was overwhelmed with fear, panic, and tremendous guilt. What had I done? I wasn't ready for a baby!

I thought your father, David, really loved me and would stand by me and marry me. Wrong. Wrong. Wrong. He got furious with me, blamed me, and worked hard to convince me to get an abortion. I do blame him for these actions, but I have forgiven him.

Bonnie, I am responsible for ending your life. I'm not going to blame David even though he played a part. It was my decision to have sex, and ultimately, it was my decision to end your life. No one could force me to go to that clinic and allow your life to be snuffed out. I did it, and I am so, so, so sorry.

I want to tell you about that horrible two hours at the clinic. David and I arrived at 2:00 p.m., and I filled out some forms. We waited in a dumpy little room with a television set that was showing some stupid soap opera. Then I was taken to the room where it happened. David stayed behind in the waiting room.

The nurse was efficient, but not friendly. She got me prepared on the table and gave me some medication for the pain. It all happened so fast from that point. The doctor came in and briefly told me what he was going to do. I didn't understand most of what he said because my head was foggy.

He told me to spread my legs, and the nurse put up a sheet so I couldn't see what he was doing. He turned on some kind of a machine, and I heard strange sounds. I didn't feel too much, just some discomfort. Then it was over, and I put my clothes back on. The nurse told me some things to do to make my recovery easier. She mentioned it wouldn't be so bad because I wasn't "so far along in the pregnancy."

Bonnie, what I did to you was terribly wrong. I killed you, and I had no right to do that. I ask you to forgive me.

I'm going to read this letter to God, to my husband (who would have been a great dad for you), my best friend, and my pastor. Then I'm going to burn it with my husband beside me. Not so I can forget you because I will never, ever forget you. But to release all my pain and guilt and move on.

My husband and I have made a donation to a local pregnancy care center in your name, Bonnie. It's a Christian place where they work with pregnant women to save their unborn babies. We will continue to make donations to this center and ones like it for as long as I live.

Bonnie, I know you're in heaven. I know I will see you again. Until that day, know that your mommy loves you. We will have an eternity to catch up and be together.

Love,
Your mom

Dear God,

It feels funny to be writing You a letter, since You already know everything I'm going to communicate. But You want us to pray, and this is kind of the same thing. I think putting my confession on paper will help heal me and bring us closer.

My heavenly Father, I have made so many mistakes in my life. I don't have enough paper to list them all. These I'm-sorry letters I've written covered the really bad, sinful things I've done to others. Thank You for forgiving me of these sins and all the others.

What I want to apologize for and confess in this letter is the way I've treated You over the years. My depression has grieved You and disappointed You, I'm sure. I've not been a joyful Christian or even a decent one. I've been focused on myself and my pain, so I haven't been an effective servant to You. I've lost so many opportunities to serve You and make a difference for Your kingdom. I'm sorry. Very sorry.

I've also been angry with You for what seems like forever. I have blamed You for all the bad things that have happened to me. I've resented You and been bitter at You. I know it's okay to express my anger and disappointment with You in a direct way, but it's not okay to harbor these feelings and let them fester. I'm sorry for my resentment and bitterness.

As Job realized at the end of his healing journey, You are God, and You can do what You want. You are a great and glorious and powerful God, and yet You are also so loving and kind and patient and forgiving. Your grace amazes me!

I'm sorry for not trusting You. I'm sorry for taking so long to reconnect with You in a close relationship.

Thank You for forgiving all these sins. Thank You for hanging in there with me and healing me through these steps of recovery. Thank You for wanting to be close to me.

I realize now that's what it's all about—being close to You and walking with You through life and serving You in a faithful way.

Do Your Work

1. How much guilt do you carry? What do you feel guilty for doing? What impact does your guilt have on you? Tell a support team member the answers to these questions.

2. Who have you significantly hurt in the past? What did you do?

3. Make a list of these people and decide the order you will address them.

4. Taking the people on your list one at a time, follow the five steps: Pray for God's forgiveness, talk out your sin with someone, write the I'm-sorry letter, mail the letter, and engage in dialogue if the other person desires it.

CHAPTER 18

HOW TO SURVIVE A LOSS: THE FOUR STAGES OF TRAUMA RECOVERY

- Ten minutes ago you were engaged to be married. That's when your fiancé told you the engagement and the relationship were over.

- When you married, it was supposed to be for the rest of your life. But your partner isn't dead, and the judge has just told you you're divorced.

- After years of pretending and denying, you're just starting to face the abuse you suffered as a child.

- You stand by the gravesite and look at the box that holds a person you love.

- You've got a spouse, kids, a home, and a stack of bills. Unfortunately your boss just informed you that you don't have a job.

- "I've got some bad news," the doctor says. "You've got a serious health problem. Here are your options."

When you experience losses like these, your mind screams out two questions: Can I survive this? How can I survive this?

Yes, you can survive. You survive a loss by successfully completing four stages of recovery. These stages are painful, time-consuming, and require a great deal of effort. But they are the keys to genuine recovery.

In chapters 14 through 17, I've already explained how you work through your unresolved past pain. In this chapter we'll look at four stages that give you a clear, concise look at the progressive nature of recovery. When you understand these stages, you'll be able to see where you are in the healing process and what work you still have to do.

Denial
This is the shock stage. "I won't believe it happened." You're stunned. Dazed. Confused. Bewildered. Your brain seems to slow down, and your sense of time is distorted. You withdraw and become isolated. It's common to fantasize that things are back to normal. You blame yourself with a lot of *if* scenarios:

- If I just hadn't had the affair.

- If I had insisted she go to the doctor.

- If I had said. . .

- If I had done things differently in the relationship.

- If only I'd urged him not to go on the trip.

These are all attempts to undo the loss and make everything okay again. This stage usually lasts several weeks to two months.

Purpose
This stage provides protection by cushioning the blow and giving you time to adjust to the loss.

Task
Your one task is to believe the loss has occurred.

Stuck in the Stage
You're stuck if you continue to deny the reality of the loss.

You work overtime, do volunteer work, and clean the home obsessively, staying so busy you don't have time to absorb the loss.

You put on a happy face and pretend everything's okay. You stand up in church and praise God for the loss four months after it happened.

You continue to beg your partner to come back.

You marry or begin another relationship immediately following the breakup.

With a straight face you tell others, "I had a perfect childhood."

Anger

This is the survival stage. "It happened, and it's not fair." Anger is the normal reaction to a threat. A major loss threatens everything you believe and everything you are. A major threat equals major anger.

In the initial part of this stage, you'll be in a rage against the one you've lost (broken relationship, divorce, separation, death) or the one who abused you (boss who fired you, a person who abused you). You'll also be in a rage against God because you're smart enough to know He's in charge and allowed the loss. Keep in mind, it's best to be honest if you feel this way, and tell God that you are angry with Him and are blaming Him. This acknowledges His sovereignty, builds your faith, and leads to a more intimate relationship with Him.

You rake those to blame over the coals. You feel perfectly justified as the righteous judge. You ask thousands of questions, most beginning with why:

- Why did this happen?

- Why now?

- Why this person?

- Why to me?

- Why not to her?

You spray your anger on innocent people around you. You're irritable, tense, impatient, and intolerant. You're a cross between Attila the Hun and a pit bull with a sore tooth. It's like having PMS and strep throat at the same time. It's common to pull back from God. Your church attendance goes down. Your devotions go down. Your prayer life goes down.

This stage usually lasts two to three months.

Purpose
This stage alerts you to a major threat and provides the energy and motivation to begin your response to the threat. Anger will not, by itself, lead to recovery, but it's a critical initial step.

Tasks
The first task is the release of most of your anger at others and God. Your anger will be connected to people. Sometimes clients tell me, "I'm not angry with anyone, just the situation." I always reply, "Baloney. You're angry with at least two people. One is the human who caused you pain. The other is God."

Your anger, legitimate or not, must be expressed. Your anger needs to be expressed in a number of ways:

- Prayer (Jeremiah, Job, David—all cried out to God);

- Physical activity, exercise;

- Writing, by way of the letters recommended in previous chapters;

- Talking with your spouse, friends, pastor, counselor, and small group members;

- Directly with those who are the source of your anger.

Your anger must be expressed so you can get to the other emotions underneath.

The second task is to take basic steps to survive and get your life moving. Anger provides the power to act. Certain vital areas of your life must be functional because you have more recovery work to do.

- Keep your job or get a job.

- Pay your bills.

- Take care of the kids.

- Reestablish relationships with old friends.

- Get back into church.

- Find a support group.

- Rebuild your life.

I had a client who was going through a nasty divorce. (Of course, all divorces are nasty.) Her husband was being mean, cruel, and vindictive. He'd call her several times a day and blast her. She would listen and take it.

I helped her get in touch with her anger so she could pull herself together, get through the divorce, and build her new life. She cut her husband off and ended communication except for the children's schedules. She got a job, found a good attorney, and arranged child care for her kids.

You need to stay in the anger stage until you've done enough to survive. If you slip into depression too soon, your recovery will be a lot harder and longer. If you missed even some of the anger you needed to experience, you'll have to go back and feel that anger and get it out.

Stuck in the Stage

You're stuck in the anger stage if you are holding onto your anger and not releasing it. Anger feels good and helps you gain some power and control. So it's not unusual to not want to give it up after the normal three months. You're holding on too long if any of the following are true:

- Your life becomes characterized by bitterness, resentment, and hostility.

- You remain focused on the person who caused your pain.

- You imagine ways of harming the person you've lost or continue to do things to harm the person.

- You talk with anyone who will listen about the person you're angry with.

- You experience physical, emotional, and spiritual problems that don't go away.

- You continue to ask the why questions.

Depression

This is the assessment stage. "It happened, and I don't know if I can go on." This is when the reality of the loss hits home. Underneath anger are always hurt, deep sadness, disappointment, hopelessness, self-blame, and guilt. You *will* experience symptoms of depression:

- fatigue;

- concentration problems;

- sleep problems (can't get to sleep, wake up and can't get back to sleep, too much sleep);

- appetite problems (eating too much or too little);

- lack of pleasure in life;

- crying;

- social withdrawal;

- feelings of worthlessness;

- suicidal thoughts (usually these thoughts are vague; if you have a strong desire and a plan or if you're thinking of a plan, get professional help immediately).

You're supposed to be depressed! It's painful, of course. But it's okay, healthy, and part of recovery. Depression is usually the longest stage. Depending on the severity of the loss and the quality of your support system, it can last five to seven months.

Your depression is healthy as long as you are still functioning at a high level, have hope you will move out of your depression in time, and can still experience pleasure in life. If you experience problems in these three areas for three consecutive weeks, seek professional help.

Purpose

This stage enables you to assess the impact of the loss on your life. Your life will not be the same, so you need time to make the necessary adjustments. Common questions include, "What does this loss mean to me?" and "What will my life be like now?"

Part of recovery is taking a hard look at your life and making necessary changes.

Tasks

The first task is to fully grieve. If you don't feel and express the hurt, it remains and does damage and keeps you depressed. You need to express your pain and grief to your spouse, trusted friends, family, pastor, Christian therapist, every person involved in the loss, and God.

Express your grief in the same ways you did your anger. If you want a great example of expressing grief, read the psalms of David. He poured out his grief and received healing.

It's often more difficult to express hurt and grief because these emotions are so tender and vulnerable. When you're angry, you feel like a massive bulldozer careening down the road. When you're depressed, you feel like you're standing out in the middle of the road alone and scared.

The second task is to gather facts. In order to assess the impact of the loss, you need all the facts. You can't recover from something you don't know about.

For example, the victim of an affair needs to find out as much as possible about the adulterous relationship: when it started, how it progressed, where they went, what they did, what they talked about, and when it ended. Go over the details until you know what happened. You want a realistic picture of the events leading up to the loss and the loss itself. Remember scenarios, events, and interactions. Talk and write them out. The more specific, the better. This is a good way to break through to the hurt and the pain. The pain and the healing are in the details.

If you have a failed relationship (breakup, separation, divorce), it's important to know just what happened. With these facts, you can fully grieve and learn from your mistakes.

The third task is to assign responsibility. What part did *you* play in the loss? Unless you were the victim of abuse or adultery, it's likely you have some responsibility. What part did others play in the loss? What part did God play? God did allow the loss.

The fourth task is to decide to go on with your life. This happens at the end of the depression stage. After you have worked through the pain, you can make a conscious choice to leave the pain and misery and live in a new, healthier way.

Stuck in the Stage
You're stuck in the depression stage if you remain depressed and your life is not beginning to move in positive, healthy directions. Your depression may be obvious if a number of symptoms are clearly present. Your depression may have more subtle symptoms: Your life lacks goals, direction, and meaning; you feel emotionally flat and numb; you develop a negative, critical attitude.

Acceptance
This is the growth stage. "It happened, and I'll learn to live with it."

You're never the same, but you go on. The loss will always be remembered and felt to a degree, but your growth and the changes pull you through to a better life.

Your mood lifts, and you feel better about life and yourself. Your activity level rises. You begin experiencing pleasure again. You laugh and see humor in situations. You spend more time with family and friends. You go back to old hobbies. People who know you say, "You're back to your old self."

These changes take time and effort. They do not happen overnight. This stage usually lasts three to six months.

Purpose

This stage allows you to complete the healing process by taking steps of growth.

Tasks

The first task is to talk openly and honestly about the loss. If you have healed and are moving forward, your emotions about the loss will be significantly reduced in intensity.

The second task is to forgive yourself and others for the loss. You have fully expressed your thoughts and feelings, you have dealt directly, and you have released all your painful emotions. You have done all that you can do.

Thirdly, you establish or reestablish an intimate relationship with God through Jesus Christ. In this stage, you come to know God or you come back to God. If you come back, you relate in a deeper and more intimate way. Without an intimate connection with God, your healing is incomplete.

The fourth and final task is to make specific, healthy lifestyle changes. To truly heal, you must create positive change.

Stuck in the Stage

You're stuck if you have not genuinely changed as a person, in your relationships with others, and in your relationship with God. The whole point of loss is change. Each loss ought to move you ahead in these three areas.

If you haven't taken specific steps of growth and are just treading water, you're stuck. If your spiritual life is dry, you're stuck. If you aren't experiencing real joy and peace in life, you're stuck. If you continue to repeat dysfunctional patterns in your personal life and relationships, you're stuck.

God wants you to experience positive change, and one of His main methods to promote change is loss.

Do Your Work

1. What losses have you suffered in your life?

2. According to my four-stage model, where are you in recovery from each of your losses? Ask a few people close to you where they think you are at this moment.

3. Where are you stuck? What tasks do you still have to complete to move on and totally recover?

4. Have you been angry with God about a loss? Are you still angry? What will you do to work out your anger and reconnect with God?

CHAPTER 19

THE GOOD, GODLY LIFE:
LIVE GOD'S ADVENTURE FOR YOU

There are three facts you must understand about the healing process.

First, God is ultimately responsible for the progress you've made so far in the healing of your emotional problem. You've worked hard, and God gives you credit for your efforts. But you couldn't have done it without Him. No matter how weak your faith has been, God has been working right alongside you every moment of the journey.

Second, the final step in your healing is God. God is the only one who heals physically, emotionally, and spiritually. The most important needs you have are spiritual, and God is the only one who can meet these needs.

Third, the whole point of your healing is God. God is the point of everything in the universe. Your healing is not about you. It's about God and your relationship with Him. You heal to be close to God and serve Him in the adventure He has planned for you.

Jesus Christ sums up the kind of life He wants you to live in the second of part of John 10:10: " 'I came that [people] may have life, and have it abundantly.' " What Jesus means by living abundantly is being close to Him and God the Father and serving them effectively.

God wants to do much more for you than just heal you emotionally. He desires to be in an intimate relationship with you and to empower you to do great things for Him. He's ready. He's been ready. And because most of your emotional problem is out of the way, you're ready.

James 4:8 communicates a wonderful promise: "Draw near to God and He will draw near to you." It's time to draw near to God. How do you do it? By stepping up and taking four actions.

Come to Christ

In chapter 4, I described how you begin a relationship with God. I'll go over it again briefly because it is so critically important. First Corinthians 15:3–4 tells you exactly what you need to do in order to know God: "I delivered to you as of first importance what I also received, that Christ died for our sins according to the Scriptures, and that He was buried, and that He was raised on the third day according to the Scriptures."

When you believe Jesus died on the cross for all the sins you have ever committed and ever will commit and that He was raised from the dead, and when you trust Him for the forgiveness of your sins, you are a Christian. You know God and can never lose that relationship.

Pray

Every close relationship requires time and communication. To draw close to God, you must talk to and listen to Him in prayer as you meditate and as verses from the Bible come to you every day. In fact, Paul says "pray at all times" (Ephesians 6:18).

Who is a better teacher than Jesus on how to pray to God the Father? Jesus' prayer life is described throughout the Gospels:

- Jesus got up early in the morning to pray, in fact, while it was still dark (Mark 1:35). No one was busier than Jesus, but He made time to pray. So can you.

- Jesus often withdrew to secluded places to pray (Luke 5:16). It's important to find a quiet and private place to pray.

- Jesus prayed all night before He selected His disciples (Luke 6:12–13). The truth is that Jesus prayed before every important event in His life. Pray before your important events and, occasionally, pray for an extended period of time.

- Follow the steps of the Lord's Prayer that Jesus taught His disciples (Luke 11:1–4): Praise God, confess your sins, make requests, and ask God to help you avoid temptation.

- Come to God like a child: open, humble, trusting, and with a simple faith (Matthew 19:13–15).

- Pray with one or two others because when you do this, Jesus is with you, and God the Father will answer your prayers (Matthew 18:19–20).

- When you pray, remember the death of Jesus and what it means: His body crucified for you, and His blood shed for the forgiveness of your sins (Matthew 26:26–29).

Follow these prayer principles and you will develop a deeper level of intimacy with God the Father. As you grow closer to Jesus and God, you will grow closer to the Holy Spirit. And the Holy Spirit will empower you to live a godly life. You will walk "according to the Spirit" (Romans 8:4) and be "led by the Spirit" (Romans 8:14).

Read God's Word

- Read and meditate on God's Word, and you will be healthy and prosperous: "But his delight is in the law of the LORD, and in His law he meditates day and night. He will be like a tree firmly planted by streams of water, which yields its fruit in its season and its leaf does not wither; and in whatever he does, he prospers" (Psalm 1:2–3).

- Obey God's Word and you will be blessed: "But one who looks intently at the perfect law, the law of liberty, and abides by it, not having become a forgetful hearer but an effectual doer, this man will be blessed in what he does" (James 1:25).

- Obey the word of Jesus, and God the Father will love you, and you will have a special intimacy with Jesus and God: "Jesus answered and said to him, 'If anyone loves Me, he will keep My word; and My Father will love him, and We will come to him and make Our abode with him'" (John 14:23).

Sit down with your pastor and ask him what kind of personal and small group Bible study program he recommends you follow.

Serve God

God wants you to use the spiritual gifts He has given you to serve others (Ephesians 2:10; 1 Peter 4:10). You are to use your gifts primarily in the local church (Ephesians 4:11–16) and when you do, you will grow closer in love to your fellow church members and to Jesus: "But speaking the truth in love, we are to grow up in all aspects into Him who is the head, even Christ, from whom the whole body, being fitted and held together by what every joint supplies, according to the proper working of each individual part, causes the growth of the body for the building up of itself in love" (Ephesians 4:15–16).

Do as the apostle Paul did and gently care for others "as a nursing mother tenderly cares for her own children" (1 Thessalonians 2:7).

Part of serving God is to obey Jesus' command to make disciples (Matthew 28:19). This means leading others to Jesus and helping them grow spiritually. I also firmly believe it means helping others heal emotionally. Because you have healed emotionally, you'll be able to help others heal. God will lead these individuals to you.

God loves you with a mind-boggling, amazing love. Jeremiah calls His love an everlasting love (31:3). Because He loves you so much, He has an adventure planned for your life (Romans 8:28; Jeremiah 29:11).

With God's help, you've worked hard to experience emotional freedom. You're ready now to grasp what God has always wanted for you.

It's time to start living God's adventure for you.

Do Your Work

1. Do you have a relationship with God through His Son, Jesus Christ? If not, are you ready to begin that relationship now?

2. Praying, reading God's Word, and serving God are the three areas for spiritual action mentioned in this chapter. Which area in your life needs the most improvement? What will you do to improve it?

3. What do you think your spiritual gifts are? Ask some support team members what they think your spiritual gifts are. Arrange a meeting with your pastor to ask him the same question. Then ask your pastor what area of ministry he wants you to serve in.

OTHER BOOKS BY DR. DAVID CLARKE

Men Are Clams, Women Are Crowbars:
Understand Your Differences
and Make Them Work
(a study guide for couples
and groups is also available)

A Marriage After God's Own Heart
(follow-up materials for couples
and groups is also available)

What To Do When Your Spouse Says,
I Don't Love You Anymore:
An Action Plan to Regain
Confidence, Power, and Control

Parenting Isn't for Superheroes:
Everyday Strategies for Raising Good Kids

The Total Marriage Makeover:
A Proven Plan to Revolutionize Your Marriage

Cinderella Meets the Caveman:
Stop the Boredom in Your Marriage
and Jump Start the Passion

To schedule a seminar or order
Dr. Clarke's resources please contact:

DAVID CLARKE SEMINARS
www.davidclarkeseminars.com
1-888-516-8844

or

Marriage & Family Enrichment Center
6505 North Himes Avenue
Tampa, FL 33614